book of the year

1874

by Dr H E Priestley

Kenneth Mason

Printed by Coasby Plus Ltd
Southsea.

ISBN 085937 029 1

introduction

On May 24, 1874, Queen Victoria celebrated her 55th birthday; her son
Edward Prince of Wales (later Edward VII) was 33 on November 9 and his
second son George (later George V) was 9 on June 3. Apart from these the
most notable dates in the Royal calendar were the marriage of the Queen's
second son Alfred Ernest, Duke of Edinburgh (d 1899) to Marie
Alexandrovna, daughter of Czar Alexander II of Russia, and the birth of a
son to the Duke and Duchess in October.

Unlike 1873, there were very few events of international importance
during this year, though kings and emperors still continued their courtesy
visits from one capital to another. In Britain the only minor crisis came
in April with the shocking news that her vice-consul at San Jose in
Guatemala had been given 200 lashes by order of the commandant there.
Apologies were later made and £10,000 compensation given to the vice-
consul to atone for this outrage.

Within the countries themselves however, the situation was by no means
so placid. In the first two months of the year Britain was in the throes of a
general election which put an end to the Gladstone Government and
resulted in the first Disraeli ministry. In Germany the laws against the
Church were being rigidly enforced, resulting in the imprisonment of
several bishops, and in occasional disorder among church congregations. In
France, attempts to restore the monarchy resulted in a motion in June in
favour of a formal recognition of the Republic. In July Marshall Bazaine,
who had been tried for his conduct during the Franco-Prussian War, escaped
from his island prison and later found refuge in Madrid. The proclamation
of Alfonso XII as King of Spain at the end of December put an end to the
hopes of the Carlists, though the fighting there continued for some months
longer. In Italy the Pope definitely decided to remain in the Vatican
Palace, and the French withdrew the vessel they had placed at his disposal

5

The Welsh Fusiliers return home amid scenes of rejoicing after fighting in the Ashanti war.

should he ever wish to leave Italy.

In the United States serious flooding devastated thousands of acres in the valley of the Mississippi and its tributaries, and there were sporadic risings of several Indian tribes. By the Poland Act in June, the administration attempted to put an end to polygamy, and late in the year the Mormon leader Brigham Young was prosecuted.

The only great celebration of the year was in Iceland where, in presence of the King of Denmark, the 1,000th anniversary of the colonisation of the Island was commemorated.

Various other parts of the world suffered either through war or devastation by the elements. The French were still occupied with the conquest of Indo-China and the Dutch were involved with the long drawn-out war in Achin in the north west of Sumatra. In the early months of the year British forces under the command of Sir Garnet Wolseley completed the conquest of the Gold Coast, and the return of the victorious general with his men was greeted with enthusiasm everywhere. At the same time the lack of rain in the Indian provinces of Bengal and Behar caused serious famine.

Apart from the change of ministry and the end of the Ashanti War, the most sensational event in Britain itself was the ending of the Tichborne Trial after 188 days, and the conviction of the claimant to 14 years' penal servitude for perjury. The main industrial disputes were a series of miners' strikes and lock-outs because of a reduction in the price of coal, the strike of lace-workers in Nottingham, of razor-forgers in Sheffield and serious agricultural disputes over wages.

Conditions in agriculture were so bad that Joseph Arch, the leader of the Agricultural Union, openly recommended emigration as a remedy, and funds were set apart by various branches to assist emigrants. Great Britain lost considerable numbers of its most promising men and women, especially from the Home Counties and East Anglia in this way and there were also calls for single young women, especially in Australia. In September 60 English Mormons left Liverpool for New York en route for Salt Lake City. One wonders where their descendants are now.

There were still ample causes for public demonstrations. Samuel Plimsol was continuing his agitation for the protection of merchant seaman; there were demands for better housing for the poor in London and elsewhere, for shorter hours in shops and factories, for the abolition of Sunday working, for Home Rule for Ireland and the liberation of the Fenian prisoners. A meeting of elementary school teachers called for the setting up of a Ministry instead of the Board of Education, and for the selection of inspectors of schools from among the ranks of practising teachers. There was much protest against the increase of ritualism in churches and in November many ritualist practices were declared illegal in the Court of Arches.

The very names of some of the societies for social advancement reveal the sad plight of the destitute and needy in that year — the Orphan Working School at Haverstock Hill; the Fitzroy Ragged School whose children were taken in vans to Buckhurst Hill for a dinner of roast beef and plum pudding; the Society of Ancient Britons which existed to educate and maintain poor Welsh children; the Watercress and Flower Girls' Mission whose object was to provide capital for them to keep their businesses going in winter, and the Home for Little Boys. Philanthropists like Baroness Burdett Coutts were encouraging working people to cultivate gardens and window-boxes, to preserve natural beauty and to protect the nests of wild birds. In October the Baroness distributed prizes at Torquay to donkey-drivers who treated their charges humanely.

Lord Shaftesbury, the most noted philanthropist of them all, seems to have travelled the length and breadth of the country, addressing meetings, giving prizes and attending committees. One wonders where, at the age of 73, he found the energy to do all he did.

London saw many changes during the year — the completion of the Chelsea embankment, the opening of the new space surrounding St Paul's

Cathedral, the opening of Leicester Square Gardens and the erection of the statues there, the Post Office Library at St Martins-le-Grand, an extension of the Metropolitan Railway, the laying of the foundation stone of a new market at Billingsgate, the opening of the City Temple near Holborn Viaduct, and the launching of a floating swimming bath to be stationed near Hungerford Bridge.

This year marked the beginning of the institution of Hospital Saturday to follow that of Hospital Sunday in the previous year. The International Exhibition at Kensington, open from Easter Monday to October 31 was pronounced a dismal failure, very few people showing any interest in it, and the foundations of Temple Bar began to sink, probably owing to disturbances of the soil arising from the construction of the adjacent Law Courts.

In January the statue of the Prince Consort was set up in Holborn, and on June 30 the first of the Parliament Square statues, that of Lord Derby, was hoisted on to its pedestal in Westminster.

The holiday spirit flourished as ever, though the Whit Monday excursionists were driven back home by sudden torrents of rain in the afternoon. In June, spectators at the new Hurlingham Club ground were thrilled by an exhibition of 'hockey on horseback' and in August an American team gave a demonstration of their game of 'Base Ball' at Lords. Holiday hooliganism had already begun, and in that month artillerymen had to be called out from Shoebury barracks to help deal with roughs assaulting fishermen at Southend. The year was not without its London tragedies, the first, the death of the 'bird man' who plunged from a balloon over Cremorne Gardens, the second the explosion of five tons of gunpowder on the canal near Regents Park.

In this year half-crowns, which had not been in circulation for use in the UK since 1850 were reissued as a result of public demand. There were great festivities at Worcester in April when the cathedral was reopened after repairs lasting 20 years and costing £100,000. The joy of the inhabitants was balanced later in the year by their disappointment when the Cathedral authorities refused to allow its use for the Three Choirs Festival. In March the Royal Gold Medal of the Royal Institution of British Architects was awarded to John Ruskin and on November 3 Sir Gilbert Scott expressed regrets at Ruskin's refusal to accept it.

There was no lack of interesting and strange happenings. In February the Aberdeen Highlanders adopted the kilt in preference to their less romantic uniform, in the hope that it would help recruiting. On Good Friday the Portuguese sailors in London Docks observed their custom of flogging an effigy of Judas Iscariot. On May Day the students of Magdalen College, Oxford, observed the ancient custom of singing a Latin hymn on top of the tower. On the same day at Ling in Austria a rise in the price of beer caused serious rioting and extensive damage.

In August the Dunmow Flitch trial was revived in that small Essex village after a lapse of four years, but it turned out one of the worst ever staged. In Skipton, Yorkshire, some 15 parishioners were charged with stoning

their vicar who had disputed payment of a gravedigger's fee.
In September an infuriated crowd in Northampton tore a balloon to pieces because, owing to shortage of gas, the balloonist could not make the advertised ascent, and in the same month the miners of Bedworth colliery, north Warwickshire, refused to go down the pit, believing that the wierd noises they had heard in the night were the cries of the Seven Whistlers, presaging disaster. In December an application was made for admission to an idiot asylum in Colchester of a poor little boy who, it was claimed, was a great-great-grandson of the novelist Daniel Defoe.
There were, many men and women born in 1874 who were destined to become famous in the present century. Among literary names are those of W Somerset Maugham, Gilbert K Chesterton, Maurice Baring,

Arrival at Gravesend of the newly married Duke and Duchess of Edinburgh.

C F G Masterman, R W Chambers, authority on literary history, Geoffrey Dawson, twice editor of the *Times,* the Canadian rhymester Robert W Service and the American poets Robert Frost and Amy Lowell.
Others born in 1874 were the actor-managers George Grossmith the Younger, Sir Nigel Playfair, and Lilian Baylis of the Old Vic, the musicians Arnold Schoenberg and Gustav Holst, the entertainers Harry G Pelissier, famous before the 1914-18 war as organizer of the 'Follies', and the escapologist Harry Houdini, the American business man J D Rockefeller, the archaeologist Howard Carter who opened the tomb of the Pharaoh Tutankhamun, the cricketer Gilbert Jessop, the pioneer of wireless telegraphy Guglielmo Marconi, the antarctic explorer Sir Ernest Shackleton, the leader of the Zionist movement Chaim Weizmann, President Herbert Hoover of the United States, W L Mackenzie King, Prime Minister of Canada, and the most famous figure of all, Sir Winston Churchill.
Among anniversaries known to have been celebrated in 1874, apart from those of the royal families of Europe and the Pope were the 500th anniversary of the death of Petrarch, the bi-centenary of the birth of the·hymn-writer Isaac Watts and the centenary of the foundation of the Royal Humane Society. On the 27th of May 1874 the people of Paisley had a general holiday to celebrate the centenary of the birth there of the poet and song-writer Robert Tannahill.
In the year ending September 30, 1873, the monks of St Bernard distributed rations and clothing to no fewer than 17,221 poor travellers, many of these being half-frozen and having to be cared for at the Hospice. To people of today who are accustomed to travelling with a minimum of risk, such figures come as something of a surprise.
It would be quite impossible in a book of this size to note all the meetings of institutions, strikes, protests, deputations, charities, minor political upheavals and disasters but the most important of these have been included where it has been possible to ascertain the exact dates.
I would like to thank the Librarian of the London Borough of Newham and his staff for the great help they have given in providing source material for this book.

january

Thursday January 1
The Queen in residence at Osborne House, Isle of Wight.
The German Emperor received congratulatory visits from the Crown
Prince, the Duke of Edinburgh and members of the Royal Family.
Post Office Library opened at St Martins-le-Grand. Conversazione held and
address given by the Postmaster-General.
Landing of British troops at Cape Coast Castle (Gold Coast) preparatory to
marching on Coomassie.
Duc de la Rochefoucauld-Bisaccia, newly-appointed French Ambassador
in place of the Duc Decazes, arrived at Albert Gate to take up office.
Mount Vesuvius showed strong symptoms of an eruption, smoke issuing in
dense quantities and subterranean sounds being heard.
Japanese clamouring for war against Korea. Civil war in Japan deemed
inevitable.
Japan. The Great Temple at Tenshlig Daijon in Jeddo (Yedo) destroyed by
fire. A huge bell ten feet high so damaged as to be rendered worthless.
Death of David Morier Evans, author and journalist, aged 54.

Friday January 2
Scotland. 'The sky was lit up for several hours by incessant flashes of
lightning. West and North islands cut off by heavy thunderstorms, Com-
munications with Mull interrupted.'
Mr Gilmore Evans, a barrister of Serjeants Inn, Chancery Lane, shot
himself with a revolver. He had just received a government appointment
worth £800 a year as Registrar of a Royal Commission. Suggested that his
brain had given way under the pressure of a severe examination he had
just undergone.
The French ambassador presented his credentials.

Opening of the Cortes at Lisbon by the King of Portugal
Reopening of the Spanish Cortes at Madrid. Senor Castelar read a message
from the Government.

Saturday January 3
General fall in the price of coal, in South Yorkshire between 1s and 3s per
ton.
W S Gilbert introduced to the boards of the Little Theatre a new five-act
comedy entitled *Charity.*
Defeat and resignation of the Castelar Ministry in Spain. Coup d'État by
General Pavia, commander of the Madrid garrison. Cortes dissolved;
Marshal Serrano became dictator.
Sir Charles Bressey, civil engineer born at Wanstead, Essex (d April 14 1951)
Death of Baroness de Clifford (Sophia Russel), aged 83.

Sunday January 4
Duke of Edinburgh arrived at St Petersburg; received by Czar and Grand
Dukes.
The Bishop of London, preaching at St Paul's, protested against a form of
religion among educated classes; 'sentimental religion which loves to dream
over devotional books, over what may be termed the poetry of Christianity.
It often leads to irreligion and vanity and seldom leads to Christ.'
Marshall Serrano formed a new government in Madrid as Chief of the
Executive Power.
A rumbling audible inside Mount Vesuvius and 'the density of smoke
indicates the proximity of fiery matter' *(Times)*
Josef Suk, Czech violinist and composer born. (died May 29, 1935)

Monday January 5
Prince and Princess of Wales arrived at Marlborough House from
Sandringham.
Lord Mayor of London presided over opening of a new Board School, York
Road, Islington, to accommodate 512 boys, 354 girls and 532 infants.
Royal Academy exhibition of 400 to 500 of Sir Edwin Landseer's works.
Edinburgh. Sir Bartle Frere delivered an address to members of the
Philosophical Institution on Dr Livingstone and his work in Africa.
Preston Horse Fair opened — 'one of the most celebrated in the North of
England.'
Coal falling in value owing to augmented supplies.
Rome. The Pope received a deputation of Irishmen when a large sum of
money was presented to His Holiness.
Death of General Sir James Chatterton bart (b 1794), veteran of the Peninsular
War and Waterloo.
Death of William Edward Nightingale, father of Florence Nightingale, aged 80.

Tuesday January 6
Prince and Princess of Wales, with the Duke of Cambridge, visit the Holborn
Theatre.
Duke of Cambridge attacked when about to enter the War Office, Pall Mall
by a man said to be a retired officer of the army. The Duke told a constable
that he considered the person 'was not right in his mind.' (His assailant
turned out to be Charles Maunsell, a retired captain).
Strike in the Nottingham lace trade had lasted 23 weeks.
Joseph Arch addressed nearly 3,000 persons at Swindon. Advocated franchise and land allowance as a means of obtaining more contented and
efficient workers.
Portsea. Aria College, for training young men for the Hebrew ministry consecrated by the Chief Rabbi Dr Adler. The cost, £20,000 liquidated by the
late Mr Lewis Aria.
Posen. Mons Lodochowski, refusing to pay fines for disregard of the German
ecclesiastical laws, had his furniture taken from the Archiepiscopal Palace.

Wednesday January 7
Prince of Wales at Osborne on a visit to the Queen previous to his departure
for St Petersburg.
Antwerp. The Captain of the *British Queen* received a gold chronometer as a
token of gratitude for his conduct in saving the crew and passengers of the
Lochearn which had collided with the *Ville de Havre,* on behalf of the
Lochearn's owners Aitken and Tilburn of Glasgow.
Death of Henry Glassford Bell, sheriff of Lanarkshire, poet and Scottish
lawyer, aged 69.

Thursday January 8
Confirmation of the Princess Beatrice at Whippingham Church, Isle of Wight.
The old iron railings measuring 370 feet, sold by auction, realised £349 5s.
They had originally been put round St Paul's Cathedral and had cost £11,202.
Bow Street. Charges preferred by the Crown against Jean Luie, a witness in
the Tichborne Case, heard.
Nottingham. End of the strike of lace-workers. They had had 3s 4d a day and
had wanted a rise of 1s 8d. Dispute referred to Alderman Vickers who gave a
rise of 25%. Eventually decided on 4s for the first six days, then 4s 6d.
Bolton, Lancs. Terrible boiler explosion at the Atlas Ironworks (Alderman
Thomas Walmsley) 6 killed; many injured.

Friday January 9
Prince of Wales unveiled statue of Prince Consort on Holborn Viaduct. After-
wards attended a dinner given at the Guildhall. HRH accompanied by Duke
of Cambridge and Lord Mayor.
Remains of Emperor Napoleon III, on first anniversary of his death, deposited
in a mausoleum erected by the Empress Eugenie, coffin being placed in a
sarcophagus presented by Queen Victoria.

Address to the jury at the celebrated Tichborne trial.

Saturday January 10
Rates of mortality for the week

Hull 18	Nottingham 24	Portsmouth 29
Leeds 18	Bristol 25	Oldham 30
Sunderland 19	London 25	Manchester 31
Sheffield 22	Norwich 25	Salford 32
Bradford 23	Liverpool 27	Birmingham 34
Wolverhampton 24	Leeds 28	Newcastle-on-Tyne 37

Prince and Princess of Wales with Prince Arthur, attended by a numerous suite, left London en route for St Petersburg.

The Empress Eugenie sent a letter to the Bishop of Troyes protesting against the prohibition of masses there for the repose of the soul of the Emperor Napoleon III.

14   General elections to German Parliament held.

Sunday January 11
Prince of Wales crossed on steamer *Samphire* to Calais and continued his journey via Brussels to Berlin.
Rain urgently needed in Bengal; famine threatened.
Bertram Hopkinson, engineer and physicist born (died 1918).

Monday January 12
Prince and Princess of Wales arrived at Berlin 7 30 am.
Received by Crown Prince and escorted to Imperial Palace.
Sheffield. Opening of Trades Union Congress. Report received that '1873 has been unparalleled for the growth of Trades Unionism.'
Paris. Vote of confidence passed by the Assembly in the ministry of the Duke de Broglie.
Genoa. The Marquise Maria Brignole Sale, last surviving branch of her family, assisted by Senators of the Kingdom, her husband and their son Marquis Filippo, gave to the City 'that palace with its magnificent library and gallery of pictures which are renowned all over Europe.' To be opened to students and visitors; revenues to be applied to encouragement of literature and art and to the purchase of artistic treasures for the City.
Washington. Bill for raising salaries of members of Congress passed in the last Session, repealed.
Surrender of Cartagena, Spain. Town occupied by the Spanish Government troops under General Lopez Dominguez.

Tuesday January 13
Prince and Princess of Wales left Berlin, evening en route for St Petersburg.
Conversazione in Mansion House on behalf of the Home for Little Boys near Farningham. Guests received by Lord Mayor and Lady Mayoress in the Salon.
National Early Closing Congress held in Manchester to support J Lubbock's Shop Hours Regulation Bill. Delegates from all principal towns. Resolutions adopted that, moral suasion having failed, every effort should be made to ensure passing of Bill.
New Year Treat to children of Great Ormond Street Hospital.
Six of crew of SS Preston sentenced to five months in prison and a stowaway fined 20s or 14 days.
New Years Day in Russia. Twenty-third birthday of Grand Duke Alexis, 3rd son of Czar. Reception of ministers by Czar.
Members of Cartagena Junta, Spain, arrived at Oran, N Africa in steamer *Numaneia* and placed themselves under French protection.
General conscription adopted in Russia.
Henry W C Davis, historian and writer, editor of the Dictionary of National Biography, born at Ebley, nr Stroud (died June 28 1928)

Wednesday January 14
Prince and Princess of Wales arrived on Russian frontier.
Bishopsgate. Crowded meeting of frequenters of Epping Forest presided over by Lord Mayor. Report read on measures taken for preservation.

Representatives of various asphalt companies held a meeting for the purpose of devising means whereby it may be rendered more safe for the traffic of horses. Agreed to offer a handsome prize for the best means of keeping road surfaces clean.
Cardinal Antonelli dangerously ill (gout in stomach). Extreme unction administered by Pope.

Thursday January 15
Prince of Wales in St Petersburg. Paid formal visit to Czar and Czarevna.
Bank rate reduced from 4% to 3½%.
Southwark. Public meeting of tradesmen to protest against price of gas.
Entry of Rifle Brigade into Ashanti territory.
Paris. Great fete at Elysée given by Marshal MacMahon to Diplomatic Body. Orleans princes and deputies of all parties present. Building illuminated

Friday January 16
Prince and Princess of Wales paid numerous visits in St Petersburg and visited opera in evening.
Dublin. Meeting in favour of Hospital Sunday. A letter read from Cardinal Cullen disapproving of the project.
Leith. Fire at flour mills of Alexander and Robert Tod. Buildings completely destroyed. £200,000 to £250,000 damage. Nearly 400 made workless.
Chairman and ex-manager of Jersey Joint Stock Bank acquitted on charge of having presented a false balance sheet to shareholders.
South Kensington Museum. Address by Frank Buckland on fish culture. He observed that it was remarkable that nearly all salmon rivers ran through cathedral towns, the obvious reason being that the monks who built the cathedrals had an eye to obtaining good fish.
Berlin. Great uproar in Prussian Parliament. Prince Bismarck denounced as an 'audacious falsehood' the accusation that he had entertained proposals for ceding territory on left bank of Rhine to France. Accusation finally withdrawn.
Rome. Cardinal Antonelli improving.
Robert William Service, poet and novelist born at Preston, Lancs (died Sept 11, 1958).

Saturday January 17
First Cabinet Council for the year held at Downing Street.
Sir Samuel Baker, the Central African explorer, entertained at a banquet by municipality of Brighton.
Sheffield. Last meeting of Trade Union Congress. Discussions on direct representation of labourers in Parliament, federation of trades unions, co-operative and industrial partnerships, technical education and international arbitration.
Heavy snowstorms reported in north of Scotland. Roads impassable.
Leith. New swing bridge opened across harbour. The iron bridge weighing 750 tons had cost £32,000.

A spectacular fire at a Leith flour mill.

Greensboro', South Carolina. Death of Siamese twins Chang and Eng; Eng lived two hours longer than Chang.

Sunday January 18
Prince and Princess of Wales with Emperor and Grand Dukes witnessed scene of 'blessing the waters of the Neva' from a pavilion on river bank, and ladies from windows of Winter Palace.
London. Mass meeting of London carmen at Hall of Service, Old Street to support an application for an advance in wages to 5d per hour for a 12 hour day, 6d for overtime and the abolition of Sunday working.
Death of Lord Blayley, Irish Representative peer, aged 71.
Death of Sir Montague John Cholmeley Bart MP for North Lincolnshire, of Easton Hall, Lincs, aged 72.

Monday January 19
Warwick. During a hunt 'the fox led the pack through the streets of this venerable city'.
Swedish Diet opened by King Oscar who spoke of friendly relations existing between Sweden and all foreign powers.
Death at Corvey in Höxter am Weser, of August Heinrich Hoffmann, German poet, philologist and literary historian. (born at Fallersleben, Luneburg, Hanover, April 2, 1798).
Paul Bruno, German architect and painter, born.

Tuesday January 20
Sir Garnet Wolseley and the Naval Brigade crossed the Prah river on their
way to Coomassie, capital of the Ashanti kingdom.
Death of H R H the Countess of Syracuse, wife of the brother of
Ferdinand II of Naples, aged 60.

Wednesday January 21
Three Tonic Solfa deputations, one from the Tonic Solfa College, one from
the Free Church Musical School and one from the Free Church Psalmody
Committee of Edinburgh, attended Mr Forster (Secretary of the Board of
Education) to complain of obstructions which they alleged were thrown
in the way of teachers trained in this system in obtaining certificates for
music.
Liverpool. T Brassey MP addressed a meeting on the importance of
increasing the volunteer naval artillery force. A fund established to equip
300 volunteers.
A deputation of 400 persons, mainly miners from the north, submitted to
Mr Gladstone their views on the desirability of extending the county
franchise.
Meeting of clergy and laity of Bath to protest against the introduction of
auricular confession into the Church of England.
Heavy rainfall in Bengal extended as far as Oudh and embraced the whole
famine area, 1½ million required famine relief. Sir Richard Temple
appointed to superintend the relief operations in the famine-stricken
districts.
Death of Lord Stuart de Decies, Lord-Lieutenant of Waterford, aged 70.

Thursday January 22
The Duke of Cambridge and the Lord Chancellor dined with the Queen at
Osborne House.
Marriage treaty between the Duke of Edinburgh and Princess Marie
Alexandrovna signed at St Petersburg.
Mansion House. 'Juvenile Ball' given by Lady Mayoress.
Truro. Total of 3,847 tons of Cornish copper realised £15,535 - 7s - 6d an
average of £4 - 1s - 0 per ton.
Birth of William Mather Rutherford Pringle, Liberal politician at Gordon,
Berwickshire, (died April 1, 1928).

Friday January 23
The Queen, accompanied by Princess Beatrice, drove through West Cowes
and Newport to view the decorations in honour of the royal marriage at
St Petersburg. Prince Leopold and the Duke of Cambridge walked through
the streets. Royal salutes fired from ships.
Marriage of the Duke of Edinburgh and Princess Marie Alexandrovna
celebrated at Winter Palace at St Petersburg 'with the utmost pomp and in
accordance with the rites of the Orthodox and Anglican Churches
respectively'.

Labourers at Sandringham on royal estate received gifts of money and a dance held in commemoration of the marriage.

Mr Gladstone announced the dissolution of Parliament and issued his address to the electors of Greenwich seeking re-election. He promised abolition of income tax.

G H Whalley MP sentenced by the Lord Chief Justice Cockburn to pay a fine of £250 for contempt of court by his proceedings in the Titchborne Case, and imprisoned in default of payment.

165th day of Tichborne trial.

The first ironclad built in Hull launched from Earle's yard. Christened by Madame Goni, wife of Admiral Goni, the *Almirante Cochrane*.

Saturday January 24

Gladstone's address to electors of Greenwich published, announcing that the Queen had been advised by her ministers to dissolve Parliament.

'Unconscious England awoke and found itself in the throes of a dissolution of a Parliament which, it had been anticipated, could have died peacefully' (Illustrated London News, January 31)

Woolwich Arsenal. A 'fish torpedo', one of the latest inventions for attacking ships under water, exploded accidentally. One man killed, five others injured.

The Lord Mayor of London announced the opening of Bengal Famine Subscription List. He had already received a cheque for £500.

Despatch from Sir Garnet Wolseley, Gold Coast. 'All the white prisoners are now in my camp. The King accepts the terms I offer; says he will pay the indemnity I demanded for £200,000'.

Death of Adam Black, publisher of the Encyclopaedia Britannica and the Edinburgh Review, formerly MP for Edinburgh. (born Edinburgh Feb 20, 1794).

Monday January 25

Calcutta. Six hours' soaking rain reported on this day; one inch in Bengal, slightly less in Bihar.

Birth of W Somerset Maugham in Paris. (died Dec 16, 1965)

Tuesday January 26

Queen held a Council; Mr Gladstone present. The eighth Parliament of Queen Victoria dissolved.

London. Ceremony of dedicating St Paul's to the public. Space surrounding the Cathedral thrown open to public — 7,000 square feet which had been purchased by the City Corporation for £15,000.

Mr Disraeli's reply to Mr Gladstone and his own election address published. Date of new Parliament fixed for March 5.

Intelligence received of death of Dr Livingstone at Ilala in Central Africa on May 4, 1873.

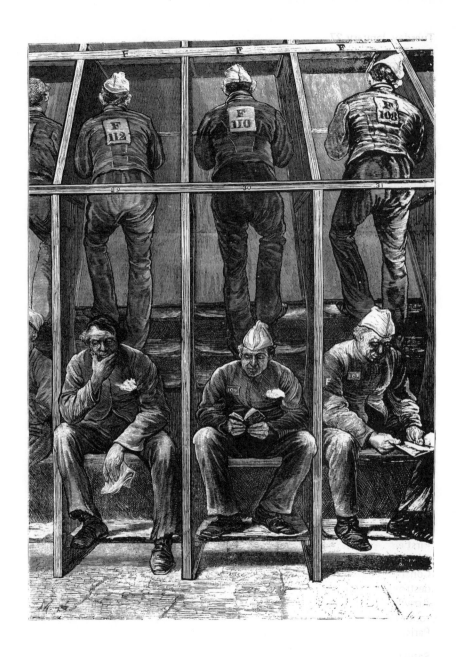

20 *The treadwheel in the Clerkenwell 'house of correction'.*

Tuesday January 27
Collision at Bo'ness Junction, on the Glasgow and Edinburgh line of the North British Railway; 15 persons killed.
Public meetings at St James's and Exeter Halls to express sympathy with Germany in its struggle against Ultramontanism.
Death of Lord St John of Bletsoe, aged 62.
Death of Admiral Thomas Gill, RN, aged 95
Death of Sir Walter Palk Carew, Bart, aged 66

Wednesday January 28
Plymouth. Shocking wife murder. Sylvanus Sweet, a man of independent means quarrelled with his wife about the use of a pomatum pot and in a fit of anger seized an old cutlass, struck her several times and she died immediately. The husband then took a cab and gave himself up at the police station.
Slave-hunting expedition into Sudan brought about a pitched battle between the Khedive of Egypt and the Sultan of Darfoor with an army of 10,000, the latter being completely routed.
Death at London of John Christian Schetky, Scottish marine painter (born Edinburgh, August 11, 1778).
Death of Sir John Kingston James, Bart, aged 59
Death of Baron Ludwig Karl Wilhelm Gablenz, Austrian Field-marshal, aged 59.

Thursday January 29
The Lord Chief Justice Cockburn commenced his charge to the jury in the Tichborne Case.
The supplementary convention between France and England respecting customs duties ratified in the French Assembly.
Cricket. England v New South Wales. England 92 and 90. New South Wales 1st innings 127, and won by 8 wickets.
Birth of John Davison Rockefeller junr at Cleveland, Ohio (died Tuscan, Arizona, May 11, 1960)

Friday January 30
First elections to the new Parliament held.
Cambridge. Eight cases of typhoid fever discovered.
Constantinople. Great fire. 100 houses including residence of Grand Vizier destroyed.
Arrival of Prince Napoleon (The Prince Imperial of France) at Milan en route for Prangins to join Princess Clothilde, then to undertake journey to Paris.

Saturday January 31
Consols, highest price 92 3/8, lowest 91 7/8.
Great battle at Amoaful near Coomassie between British forces under Sir Garnet Wolseley and Ashantees, latter defeated.
Death of Duncan McNeill, Rt Hon Lord Colonsay, Scottish judge, aged 80.

february

Sunday February 1
Oxford. Consecration of Dr Charles Waldegrave Sandford as Bishop of Gibraltar.
Sir Garnet Wolseley destroyed village of Becquah, about a mile west of Amoaful, site of battle of January 31.
Earthquake in Canada, felt at Farther Point near Quebec.
Salmon fishing opened in English and Welsh rivers.
Birth of Hugo von Hofmannsthal, Austrian poet and playwright at Vienna.

Monday February 2
Queen (at Osborne House) held a Council for the purpose of picking the Sheriffs.
Nine persons killed at Bury, Lancs, by the falling of a building in which an election meeting was being held.

Tuesday February 3
Prime Minister's constituency of Greenwich, population 170,000 — 16,000 electors polled.
Posen. Arrest and imprisonment of Archbishop Lodochowski (see Jan 6).
Death of King Lunalilo of the Sandwich Islands (Hawaii), age 39.
Gertrude Stein, American novelist born at Allegheny, Pennsylvania (died July 27, 1946).

Wednesday February 4
Duke and Duchess of Edinburgh accompanied by Czar, Cesarewitch and Czarevna with Prince and Princess of Wales arrived Moscow.
Gold Coast. Capture of Coomassie by forces under Sir Garnet Wolseley after five days' fighting.

Rain falling generally in Bengal.

Thursday February 5
Moscow. Great festivities, in honour of marriage of Duke of Edinburgh and Princess Marie Alexandrovna, who were received with great enthusiasm. Congratulated by nobility, reviewed a regiment and visited one of the monasteries.
Polling at Tower Hamlets, Southwark and Chelsea.
Opening of German Reichstag at Berlin. Speech from throne read by Prince Bismarck. Deputies from Alsace and Lorraine present for first time.
Death of the Earl of Howth KP, Lord-Lieutenant, county Dublin, aged 71.
Death of Moritz Haupt, German philologist, (born Zittau, Lusatia, July 27, 1808).

Friday February 6
Duke and Duchess of Edinburgh drove out and visited places of interest in Moscow.
City of London elections; return of three Conservatives and one Liberal.
Streets of Commassie cleared by Naval Brigade previous to setting town on fire. British forces began their return march to the coast.
Death of John Pye, one of the foremost landscape painters of his time, aged 92.
Death of General Sir J Gaspard le Marchant KCB, GCMG, Colonel, 11th Foot, aged 71.

Saturday February 7
London. Performance of Gounod's *Jeanne d'Arc* which had been produced at the Paris Gaieté Theatre in autumn, 1872. Given and conducted by the composer for the first time in England at the first of the series of Gounod concerts.
Morning performance of *The Rivals* at the Gaiety.
John Wilkinson, proprietor of the Oakenshaw Print Works, Clayton-le-Moors near Accrington, caught by some revolving machinery in his own establishment. 'Before the engine could be stopped his life was gone, his body being frightfully mutilated.'
Melbourne cricket: English XI, 406; combined XV of Australia, 189.
Rome Carnival inaugurated.
Death of Baron Meyer Amschel de Rothschild, late MP for Hythe, aged 56.

Sunday February 8
Duke and Duchess of Edinburgh arrived back at St Petersburg at 11 am.
Death of Herman Merivale CB, Under-Secretary of State for India, aged 67. (Born Dawlish, November 8, 1806).
Death of David Friedrich Strauss, theological writer, author of 'Life of Jesus' etc, aged 65. (Born Ludwigsburg, nr Stuttgart, Germany, Jan 27, 1808).

Monday February 9
Royal Geographical Society. Sir Bartle Frere (British administrator), speaking on the question of the fate of Dr Livingstone, said that while a ray of hope still remained, it was very small indeed.
Death at Hyeres of Jules Michelet, French historian, born Paris, August 21, 1798.
Birth, at Brookline, Mass, of Amy Lawrence Lowell, poet and critic (died May 12, 1925).

Tuesday February 10
Meeting at Mansion House to authorise public subscription for Bengal Famine Fund.
Barque *Lady Havelock* of Liverpool wrecked on Goodwins. Master and crew of 15 saved by lifeboat *Bradford* and taken to Ramsgate harbour.
Bengal. Allahabad. All institutions giving relief crowded.

From an artist's sketchbook — a naval brigade clearing the streets of Coomassie during the Ashanti war.

Moorshedabad — labourers getting one meal a day. Behar — prices doubled.
Great privation everywhere.
Birth at Narborough, Leics, of Sir Robert Sangster Rait, historian and
Principal of Glasgow University (died May 25, 1936).

Wednesday February 11
Duke and Duchess of Edinburgh present at keel laying of an ironclad corvette
to be named *Duke of Edinburgh.*
Visit of Prince of Wales and Crown Prince of Germany to Cronstadt.
Departure of Emperor of Austria from Vienna on a visit to Emperor of Russia
at St Petersburg.
Exeter Hall. Meeting of Friends of movement for advancing wages and
abolition of Sunday duty in minor departments of Postal Service. Mr Antony
J Mundella in chair. Many other MP's present.
Schleswig-Holstein. High tide overflowed entire coast. Dykes broken.

Thursday February 12
Mr Benjamin Disraeli re-elected to Parliament for Buckinghamshire.
David Katakaua elected King of the Sandwich Islands. Age 37.
Opposed by adherents of Queen Emma, who attacked and set fire to House of
Assembly, wounding several members. Attackers dispersed by British and
American sailors and marines from HMS *Tenedos* and US vessels *Benicia*,
Tuscarra and *Portsmouth.*
Death of Francis Smith, introducer of screw-propeller into Royal Navy,
aged 66.

Friday February 13
Burning of Belgrave Pentechnicon, a miscellaneous repository for property
of all descriptions. Of vast size, built round four sides of an open yard and
five to six storeys high. Much valuable property lost.
Envoy of King Koffee of Ashanti received by Sir Garnet Wolseley at Fomena
suing for peace. Draft treaty sent to Coomassie for signature.
Prince Arthur arrived at Berlin from St Petersburg on his way to England.
Emperor of Austria arrived at St Petersburg. Duke and Duchess of Edinburgh
present at welcoming ceremony.

Saturday February 14
Queen still at Osborne House.
Close of the principal elections, results showing great gains for the Conser-
vative party.
Herr Joachim, the great violinist appeared at Crystal Palace and played
Spohr's 7th Concerto in E Minor.
'Splendid saloon carriage' specially constructed by GWR for Her Majesty's
journeys between London and Gosport taken out for a trial trip and 'gave
perfect satisfaction.'
Cricket in Australia. England v the Twenty-two of Bendigo. England won
by 7 wickets.

Hussein Avni Pasha appointed Grand Vizier of Turkey.

Sunday February 15
London. Fire in Carnaby Street. Two dead.
Mr Jefferson Davis arrived at Liverpool from New Orleans, having been
directed by his physician to take a sea voyage for the benefit of his health.
Spain. Carlists began the bombardment of Berga.
Death of Cardinal Tarquini who had recently been created cardinal, at
Rome. Aged 54.
Birth at Kilkee, Co Kildare of Sir Ernest Henry Shackleton, explorer of
South Polar regions. (Died May 5 1922).

Monday February 16
Meeting at Mansion House under presidency of Lord Mayor of London to
open subscription list for relief of sufferers from famine in Bengal. Sub-
scription of £1,000 from Queen reported.
Meeting of Cabinet Council at Downing Street to consider political
situation.
London. Meeting of railway directors, officers and shareholders in Cannon
Street. Movement set on foot for procuring repeal of passenger duty (5
per cent on 1st and 2nd class fares).
Berlin. Fifteen deputies from Alsace and Lorraine took their places in the
Reichstag on the extreme Right.
Brussels. Death of Lambert Adolphe Jacques Quetelet, Belgian astronomer,
founder and director of the Brussels Observatory. (Born at Ghent, February
22, 1796). Britannica puts Quetelet's death on February 17. Whittaker and
Illustrated London News on February 16.

Tuesday February 17
Queen left Osborne, Isle of Wight, for Windsor by way of East Cowes, taking
the Royal Yacht Albert to Gosport, then by way of Royal Saloon Carriage,
recently built at GWR works at Swindon, via Winchester, Basingstoke and
Reading to Windsor. Arrived Windsor 1.20.
Afternoon, Mr Gladstone had audience of the Queen at which he tendered
his resignation and that of his ministers. Queen sent for Mr Disraeli.
Melbourne. Col Egerton Warburton arrived after having left Tennants Creek,
Adelaide, 12 months previously *(Times)*.
Constantinople. Grand Ball at French Embassy. Grand Vizier, main foreign
residents and some 500 guests present.
First day of Chinese New Year. All quiet in Peking.

Wednesday February 18
Queen visited by Rt Hon W E Gladstone and Rt Hon Benjamin Disraeli.
Mr Disraeli in obedience to a royal summons waited on Queen and received
Her Majesty's command to form a cabinet.
Sixteen representative peers of Scotland elected at Holyrood to sit in the new
Parliament.

A youth of 17 years of age sentenced to one month's imprisonment for throwing a ginger-beer bottle from the gallery of the Elephant and Castle Theatre and injuring an occupant of the pit.

Berlin. Deputies from Alsace-Lorraine applied for permission to speak in French. Request refused. Motion for a plebiscite in Alsace-Lorraine rejected and Alsace-Lorraine members marched out of Reichstag in a body.

Paris. Mme MacMahon addressed members of Paris press on misery prevalent in various quarters and on the necessity for abundant relief. Sum of 200,000 francs required.

Thursday February 19

Rugby School. Governing body met to choose a headmaster in succession to Dr Hayman, dismissed on December 19, 1873. Rev Thomas William Jex-Blake DD, Principal, Cheltenham College, appointed.

Large meeting of ladies and gentlemen at Cannon Street Hotel to sample meat, geese, turkey, chicken etc brought from banks of Danube and saleable at half normal prices viz: mutton 3½d per lb retail, goose 2/3d each, turkeys 2/9d, chicken 6d, Transylvanian honey 8d per lb.

Friday February 20

The Queen had audience of Mr Disraeli who kissed hands as First Lord of the Treasury. Mr Gladstone had audience of the Queen and delivered up the seals as Chancellor of the Exchequer and First Lord of the Treasury. Disraeli Cabinet of 12 members completed.

Sir Garnet Wolseley's small force crossed River Prah and pushed on to Coomassie.

Accident to the Scotch Limited Mail at Euston; two deaths caused by injuries.

A comet discovered by Professor Winnecke, Director of the Observatory at Strasburg at 17h 40 GMT.

Death of Robert White, border poet and historian, aged 72.

Birth at Keighley, Yorks of Gordon Bottomley, author, dramatist and poet (died August 25, 1948)

Saturday February 21

Queen held two councils, one of the outgoing, the other of incoming ministers.

Replies received to the Master of the Mint's circular of December 31 shows strong favour of concurrent circulation of the crown and the florin. The issue of half-crowns announced 'with as little delay as possible.' (There had been no half-crowns issued for use in UK since 1850);

Birth at Islington of Dame Lilian C Barker, first woman assistant prison commissioner (died May 21, 1955).

Sunday February 22

Prince Arthur arrived at Windsor Castle from Russia, attended divine service with Princess Beatrice, and later left for Aldershot to assume duties of

Striking a bargain at a fashionable charity bazaar.

Brigade-Major of 1st Infantry Brigade.
Spain. Bombardment of Portugalete by Spanish squadron. Carlists commenced bombardment of Bilbao.

Monday February 23
The new ship Hesperus, 1700 tons, sailed for Adelaide. Besides passengers and cargo, it had on board 416 emigrants equal to 348 statute adults. These had been carefully selected and comprised people of all industrial occupations besides 45 single domestic servants.
Arrival of Emperor of Austria at Moscow; city illuminated.
Death of Charles Shirley Brooks, editor of *Punch,* humorist and novelist;

'one of the few literary men of our time who have cultivated letter-writing as an art' (Illustrated London News). Born April 29, 1826, in London.

Tuesday February 24
Archbishop of York presided at inaugural meeting of Hull Branch of Seamen's Mission.

London. Meeting held at Watercress and Flower Girls' Mission, Laystall Street, in connection with Emily Loan Fund: President, Earl of Shaftesbury. Object — 'to advance this poor class of the community the small capital they may require to set them up in business during the winter'. (Already nearly 300 poor street hawkers had been assisted and many thus kept from pauperism).

The *Murillo* which had run down and sunk the *Northfleet* (see January 22, 1873) left Cowes Roads en route from Cadiz to Hamburg. Had been re-christened the *Huelva*.

Samuel Plimsoll presented with an illuminated address by a deputation of sailors plying between London and Hamburg to show their admiration of his conduct on their behalf.

Emperor of Austria left Moscow for Warsaw.

General Moriones defeated near Bilbao three times with great loss in efforts to force entrenchments of Carlists.

Death of the Rev Thomas Binney DD, eminent nonconformist divine (born at Newcastle-on-Tyne in 1798).

Wednesday February 25
Her Majesty, accompanied by Princess Beatrice, left the Castle for London by special train to Paddington, escorted from there to Buckingham Palace by detachment of 1st Life Guards.

First Cabinet Council of Disraeli Ministry. All ministers present.

Brigantine *Lizzie* of Swansea run down in morning near Lands End by steamer *Broomsgrove* of Southampton. All the crew saved.

Board school for nearly 1100 children opened in Westmoreland Road, Walworth, London. Cost, £13,561.

Paris. Reception of M Emile Ollivier (Former Prime Minister of France) at the French Academy.

Birth at West Bromwich of Sir Robert M Hodgson, diplomatist (died October 18, 1956).

Thursday February 26
Resolution by Court of Common Council to present Freedom of City of London in a gold box value 100 gns to Sir Bartle Frere in testimony of his long and honourable career in India.

Death at Berlin of Johann Georg Ludwig Hesekiel, German author, song-writer and novelist (born August 12, 1819 at Halle).

Friday February 27
Professor Thomas Huxley installed as Lord Rector of University of
Aberdeen.
With view to increased popularity and promotion of recruiting, Royal
Aberdeenshire Highlanders adopted the kilt in lieu of their former less
picturesque uniform.
Paris. The French Court of Appeal gave judgment against Naundorff,
the Bourbon claimant, who had sued the Comte de Chambord as
grandson of the Dauphin of France.
Marshal Serrano appointed President of the Spanish Executive Power. Left
Madrid to command the army of the North.
Birth at Eastborne of Francis M Cornford. Classical scholar (died
Jan 3, 1943).

Saturday February 28
Duke and Duchess of Edinburgh left St Petersburg en route for England.
Enormously lengthy trial of Thomas Castro, alias Arthur Orton, claimant
to the Tichborne Estates and title for perjury, concluded in Court of
Queen's Bench after 188 days' sittings begun on April 23, 1873. 'The
prisoner now wears prison dress, has the prison diet and is employed
picking oakum.' Sentence — 14 years.
Regent Street, Westminster. Fancy bazaar held in a hall built by a
number of working men by means of small subscriptions for a Working
Men's Club, with reading and refreshment rooms and a lecture hall. Cost
£200. Accommodation 600 - 700. Cost subscribed entirely by the working
classes.
London. The 159th anniversary festival of the Society of Ancient Britons
celebrated at Willis's Rooms. Object — education and maintenance of poor
Welsh children. 'At present there are 112 boys and 45 girls in the school
enjoying the benefits of charity.'
Total of 3251 emigrants left for New Zealand in this month alone. Also
5590 persons emigrated from England by way of Liverpool — 322 fewer
than in February 1873; 4838 of the latter went to US.
South Africa. Disturbances in Natal. 'Small bands of rebels lurk in the
mountain gorges but are being vigorously hunted.'
Mount Vesuvius covered with snow from summit to base.
Consols; highest price 92 3/8, lowest 91 7/8.
Death of Duchess of Buckingham and Chandos.

march

Sunday March 1
Prince and Princess of Wales arrived at Berlin (morning). Emperor of
Germany not present owing to delicate health.
Pope received members of a club representing associations devoted to
Catholic interests and also gave audience to several members of English
Catholic families.
Birth at Edinburgh of Sir Arthur G Wauchope, soldier and administrator
(died September 14, 1947).

Monday March 2
Queen held council at Buckingham Palace. Prince Arthur, the Duke of
Abercorn, Mr Disraeli and others present.
Duke and Duchess of Edinburgh arrived at Berlin. Prince and Princess
of Wales present at reception of Duke and Duchess.
Conference of representatives of working men of West of England and
South Wales at Tailors' Hall, Bristol in connection with Workmen's Peace
Association. Resolutions in support of principle of international
arbitration.
London. Festival of hairdressers held in small concert room, Hanover
Square Rooms 'to afford 16 members of the profession an opportunity to
exhibit their skill.'
Conversazione to celebrate completion of building of new Dental Hospital,
Leicester Square.
Liverpool new Central Railway Station opened for traffic.
House coal in Durham coalfields reduced by 3s to 4s per ton.
A tremendous gale washed over decks of British steamer *Laconia* on
voyage between Alexandria and Tunis with pilgrims on board; 117 reported
drowned.

31

Death of Dr Neil Arnott FRS Physician Extraordinary to the Queen aged
86. (born Arbroath May, 1788).
Birth at Barlaston, N Staffs of Sir Ralph Wedgwood, railway administrator
(died September 5, 1956).

Tuesday March 3
Duke and Duchess of Edinburgh visited places of interest in Berlin.
Left at midnight for Verviers.
Duke of Abercorn arrived in Dublin to be sworn in as Lord-Lieutenant of
Ireland.
The Prince Imperial of France received a number of Bonapartists at
Camden House, Chislehurst, and received a bouquet.
Death of Dr Forbes Benignus Winslow, physician and authority on
diseases of the brain, aged 64.
Birth of Ada Crossley, operatic singer at Gippsland, Australia (died
October 17, 1929).

Wednesday March 4
Duke and Duchess of Edinburgh received at Verviers by British and
Russian Ministers; escorted in special train to Brussels and met by King
of Belgians.
Birth in N London of Sir Charles Herbert Reilly, Professor of Architecture
died Februay 2, 1948.

Thursday March 5
Prince and Princess of Wales arrived at Dover and travelled by South
Eastern Railway to London.
Duke and Duchess of Edinburgh with Belgian Court attended performance
at a theatre and a court dinner.
Opening of the new Parliament by royal commission.
Mendelssohn's *St Paul* performed for the first time by Royal Albert Hall
Choral Society, Conductor Dr Barnby, Dr Stainer at the organ; Soloist
Mr Sims Reeves.
Jean Luie (witness in Tichborne Case) charged with perjury and
committed for trial.
Death of Field Talfourd, portrait and landscape painter (born 1815)

Friday March 6
Duke and Duchess of Edinburgh inspected chief objects of interest in
Brussels, left for Ostend to join yacht Victoria and Albert.
Prince of Wales took his seat in the House of Lords.
Death of Countess Danner, morgantic widow of King Frederick VII of
Denmark.

Saturday March 7
Duke and Duchess of Edinburgh arrived Gravesend, proceeded to Windsor;
met by assemblage of numerous members of Royal Family.

Emperor of Germany still indisposed but able to confer with ministers.
Drove out for first public appearance since illness.
Cholera reported in Buenos Aires.

Sunday March 8
Austrian Emperor arrived at Pesth, Hungary, from Vienna. Rioting in the
city. Town Hall set on fire by populace, on reports that a prisoner had
committed suicide as result of ill-treatment.
Foundering of steamer *Tacna* on coast of Chile; 19 passengers and crew
drowned.
Death of Millard Fillmore, ex-President of the United States at Buffalo.
(born Summerhill, Cayuga County, NY, Jan 7, 1800).

Monday March 9
State banquet given by Queen at Windsor Castle in St George's Hall in
honour of Duke and Duchess of Edinburgh.
Eleventh anniversary of wedding of Prince and Princess of Wales.
Meeting of Bengal Famine Relief Fund. Amount subscribed had reached
£42,000.
Meeting of RIBA recommended that Royal Gold Medal for 1873-4 be
awarded to John Ruskin MA, Slade Professor of Fine Art at University of
Oxford.

Tuesday March 10
Queen accompanied by Prince and Princess of Wales and Duke and
Duchess of Edinburgh, with other members of Royal Family, drove to the
meet of H M staghounds at Winkfield Church 'where a fashionable field
was assembled.'
Evening. Queen held court at Buckingham Palace, Royal Princes,Prince
Christian of Schleswig-Holstein, Duke of Teck, Maharajah Duleep Singh
and others present. Sir Garnet Wolseley presented to the Queen the
Royal State Umbrella taken from the King of Ashantee's Palace at
Coomassie.
The Earl of Dudley and other coalowners in South Staffordshire reduced
coal by 4s to domestic consumers and 3s to ironmasters.
Forest of Dean coalowners reduced wages by 20 per cent. Bristol owners
agreed to arbitration.
Birth at Lustdorf, Nr Odessa of William Wolcot, architect and graphic
artist (died May 21, 1943).

Wednesday March 11
Prince of Wales held levee at St James's Palace on behalf of Her Majesty.
Over 300 presentations made to Prince.
Death of Charles Sumner at Washington through over-exertion in Senate.
(born Boston, Massachusetts January 6, 1811).
Birth at Highgate, London of Sara Margery Fry, reformer; (died April
21, 1958).

Regent Street, London gaily decorated for a Royal procession.

Thursday March 12
Public entry of Duke and Duchess of Edinburgh into London accompanied by the Queen. Escorted in semi-state to Buckingham Palace amid much popular enthusiasm.
Wreck of steamer Queen Elizabeth at western end of Gibraltar Bay while on voyage from Calcutta to London, 23 drowned.

Friday March 13
Queen held levee at Buckingham Palace for special purpose of presenting the Corps Diplomatique, Her Majesty's Household and other distinguished persons in the country to the Duchess of Edinburgh.
Reported that losses on steamer *Laconia* (see March 2) had been greatly exaggerated, only 9 persons being missing.

Saturday March 14
End of exhibition of Sir Edwin Landseer's works at Burlington House.
James Brown, eating-house keeper of Shadwell, charged at Bow Street with perjury in connection with Tichborne case.
Lockout of labourers reported in Fens and Eastern Counties. Due in some

districts to demands for more pay, in others to farmers' attempts to
reduce wages.
Treaty of Fomena ended Ashanti War.

Sunday March 15
Demonstration in Hyde Park demanding amnesty for Fenian prisoners.
Procession of 600 to 700 persons from Trafalgar Square with flags and bands
of music through West End to Reformers' Tree in Hyde Park. Huge meeting:
resolution to request Prime Minister to advise Queen to grant amnesty to
40 prisoners.
France assumed protectorate over Annam (South-east Asia).

Monday March 16
The 18th birthday of Prince Imperial. Bonapartist demonstration at
Camden House, 6,000 present.
Shaftesbury. New cottage Hospital opened in memory of late Marquis of
Westminster by Bishop of Salisbury. Cost about £2,000; erected by public
subscription on land given by Marchioness.
Professor Huxley gave first of series of six lectures on the phenomena of
life as motion and consciousness in theatre of School of Mines, Jermyn
Street. Audience composed entirely of working men.
Reduction of 2s per ton quoted on Coal Exchange.
Death of Hon Right Rev Charles Amyand Harris, late Bishop of Gibraltar,
aged 62.

Thursday March 17
Queen held a council. Rt Hon B Disraeli, Marquis of Hertford, Rt Hon R A
Cross, Lord John Manners and others present.
St Patrick's day. All passed quietly in the large towns of Ireland.
Lincoln. Gerard Maurice Burn, a boy who recently fought a duel with
intent to do grievous bodily harm, had made bullets in a mould to be fired
from a popgun such as were ordinarily sold in toyshops. His opponent was
a boy of ten. Judge and jury were all boys. Verdict — not guilty.

Wednesday March 18
The 26th birthday of Princess Louise (Marchioness of Lorne). Band of
Grenadier Guards (Director Dan Godfrey) serenaded under her window
in the morning.
W E Forster presided at annual meeting of Charity Organisations Society.
Nearly 15,000 cases had been considered during the year.
London School Board Meeting. Sum of £500 reported to have been
received from Mr Francis Peek to be expended in one year in defraying
cost of examinations in the bible and in the principles of religion and
morality in Board Schools.

Thursday March 19
Queen's speech read to the Houses of Parliament by Royal Commission.

Prince and Princess of Wales present in debate at House of Lords.
Evening. Royal Albert Hall performance of Mr Arthur Sullivan's oratorio
The Light of the World. Prince and Princess of Wales present.
James Brown, witness in Tichborne Case, committed for trial on a charge
of perjury. Bail — two sureties of £500 each.
Deputation to the Rt Hon R A Cross, Home Secretary, on the necessity of
reducing working hours of women and children in factories.
Poplar. German frigate *Kaiser* built by Samuda Bros for German Imperial
Government launched at the shipbuilders' yard by Countess Marie Munster.
Many distinguished persons present.

Friday March 20
Highest tide seen in Thames for many years; water rose to about 4 ft above
usual height. Many houses in Lambeth, Blackfriars and Vauxhall Bridge
districts flooded.
Landing at Portsmouth of 23rd Welsh Fusiliers, back from Ashanti War.
Presented by people of Portsmouth with a goat with gilt horns to replace
original goat presented by Her Majesty which had died on Gold Coast. Its
head was handed by the officers to Mr Emmanuel Hard of Portsea to be
stuffed and mounted as a regimental memento of the war.

A welcome home for the troops who fought in the Ashanti war.

Saturday March 21
Queen received a deputation from Mayor and Corporation of Windsor congratulating her on marriage of Duke of Edinburgh.
Short trial trip made from St Pancras to Bedford of a train of 'Pullman's Palace Cars' which had been placed by Midland Railway directors on their line. Two were parlour and two drawing room and sleeping cars. Result very satisfactory.

Sunday March 22
Queen at Windsor Castle received Major General Sir Garnet Wolseley CB.
Emperor William I of Germany's 77th birthday. Recovering slowly from recent illness.
Death of Albert Way MA, FSA. Founder of Archaeological Institute of Great Britain, aged 69.

Monday March 23
Queen travelled by special train to Paddington en route for Buckingham Palace.
Wigan. Conference of Miners. Proposal for a joint committee of masters and delegates to negotiate compromise on wages.
Return of 42nd Highlanders from Ashanti War to Portsmouth.
Rome. The 25th anniversary of King Victor Emmanuel's accession. City gaily decorated. General holiday. Two counter-demonstrations in honour of the Pope.

Tuesday March 24
Mr Fothergill MP, presiding over a meeting of coalowners at Cardiff, discussed an application which had come from miners to restrict output of coal in order to avoid necessity of reducing wages. This was refused.
Oldham district colliers decided to resist attempted reduction of wages; 1,800 men and boys on strike. Prospect of general strike of colliers in Black Country consequent on threatened reduction in wages.
About 1,200 locked-out agricultural labourers paraded streets of Newmarket.
Arrest of Captain Hyde of the *Tacna* by the Chilean authorities (See Sunday, March 8).

Wednesday March 25
The Queen held a 'drawing room' at Buckingham Palace. Many members of Royal Family present. For all guests this was a 'collar day' when insignia worn.

Thursday March 26
Queen left Buckingham Palace for Windsor by train. Prince of Wales held levee at St James's Palace on behalf of Queen.
Royal National Lifeboat Institution Jubilee Meeting (50 years) held at London Tavern. Duke of Northumberland in Chair.

Deputation to Mr Cross with regard to reducing hours of labour for women and children. Promised careful consideration.

Friday March 27
HMS *Rifleman* and HMS *Philomel,* with *Hugh Rose* of Bombay Marine Service, reduced fort of Maasnah on Batinah Coast, Gulf of Oman after days spent in negotiations. Rebel chief had plundered goods of some British subjects. No damage done to village.
Death of Sir William Henry Elliott KCB, Colonel 31st Regt Veteran of Peninsular War, Waterloo and Second Burmese War, aged 81.
Birth at San Francisco of Robert Frost, poet (died January 29, 1963).

Saturday March 28
Queen at Windsor Castle
Mr Samuel Plimsoll MP presented with an address from various trades in Liverpool in honours of his work for seaman.
South Staffordshire miners' strike spreading. Prospect still remained of general strike throughout Black country.
University Boat Race won by Cambridge.
English Cricket Eleven, having won by an innings at Adelaide, embarked for home.
United States. Bill passed in Congress limiting greenback issue to 400 million dollars. Protest meeting in New York against inflation of currency.
Achin, Sumatra. Dutch fortifying themselves in Achin, preparing for recommencement of operations in October with a new expedition.
Death at Gotha of Peter Andreas Hansen, Danish astronomer (born Dec 8, 1795 at Tondern, Schleswig).
Birth at Bombay of Shapuri Saklatvala, politician and communist MP in House of Commons. (died January 19, 1936).

Sunday March 29
Queen, Duke of Edinburgh, Princess Beatrice and Prince Arthur, attended divine service in private chapel at Windsor Castle.
Dr Butler, Head of Harrow School officiated.
Earthquake shock felt in Algiers.

Monday March 30
Queen, accompanied by Princess of Wales, Duchess of Edinburgh, Princess Louise, Princess Beatrice and Prince Leopold reviewed in Green Park, Windsor, 1600 men who had taken part in Ashanti War under command of Sir Garnet Wolseley.
Meeting of Indian Relief Committee at Mansion House presided over by Lord Mayor of London.
Fire at Bicton, seat of Lady Rolle near Exmouth. Many works of art lost.
Sheffield. Goods of Rev Giles Hester, a nonconformist minister seized and sold, he refusing to pay school rate on ground of conscience, objecting to 25th clause of the Education Act.

The Universities boat-race: weighing the crew.

Tuesday March 31
Consols. Highest price 92¼. lowest 91¾.
Report appeared that water drawn from Thames and Lea in March 'much polluted with organic matter'. All water supplied by all other concerns including Kent, New River and West Middlesex 'slightly turbid and not fit to be used for dietetic purposes.'
Intelligence received of escape of Henri Rochefort, French radical politician and other prisoners from New Caledonia and their arrival in Sydney, Australia.
Roman Catholic Archbishop of Cologne arrested.
Death of Marquis of Downshire, aged 29.

april

Wednesday April 1
Birthday of Prince Bismarck (born April 1 1815)
Treaty of commerce and navigation between France and Russia signed at St Petersburg.

Thursday April 2
About 1,000 miners in South Staffordshire determined not to accept reduction in wages. Resolution passed that 'although we detest strikes, yet we cannot in honour consent to the present reduction but are willing to submit the same to arbitration.'
Birth at Altrincham, Cheshire, of Ernest W Barnes, Bishop of Birmingham, author and publicist (died November 29, 1953).

Friday April 3
Good Friday. Heavy rain. Cold and boisterous wind.
Portuguese sailors at London Docks observed custom of flogging and contemptuously treating an effigy of Judas Iscariot, the false Apostle.
The *Devonshire* sailed from Gravesend with 428 emigrants bound for Queensland.
Mr Rumbold, British Minister in Chile, demanded release of Captain Hyde and an indemnity of £25,000 (see March 8 and 24).

Saturday April 4
Queen at Osborne House for Easter.
Hoxton. The wife of a tradesman named Newman murdered her infant daughter, wounded her brother and then made an attempt on her own life. It was believed that she was suddenly seized with a fit of homicidal mania, the result of grief for the death of five of her infant children

within a comparatively short period.
Death of Charles Ernest Beule, French archaeologist and politician
(born at Saumur, June 29, 1826).

Sunday April 5
Easter Day.
Her Majesty, Prince Beatrice, Prince Leopold attended divine service at
Whippingham Church, Isle of Wight. Revs George Prothero and William
Gray officiated.
Prince and Princess of Wales attended service at Sandringham Church.
Rev W Lake Onslow officiated.
Duke and Duchess of Edinburgh present at an organ performance at the
Royal Albert Hall.
Death of Commander Richard James Morrison, Commander RN,
mathematician and astrologer, editor of 'Zadkiel's Almanac' (born
June 15, 1795).

Monday April 6
Easter Monday. Metropolitan lines crowded; river steamboats, omnibuses
and tramways not sufficient to meet requirements. All well-known open
spaces filled with visitors; 48,000 at Crystal Palace, 40,000 at Zoological
Gardens, 14,000 at British Museum, 30,000 at South Kensington Museum,
13,437 at Brighton Aquarium, 7,000 to 8,000 at Albert Hall where a
Grand Military Concert with band and vocal music was given in afternoon.
Annual congress of delegates from Co-operative Societies opened at
Halifax.
Sheffield. Razor-forgers went on strike for increase in wages.
Miners' delegates in Glasgow agreed to accept reduction of 20 per cent in wages.
South Kensington. International Exhibition of 1874 opened without
ceremony; 14,000 present.
Birth at Budapest of Harry Houdini (Erich Weiss), entertainer and
escapologist, (died October 31, 1926).

Tuesday April 7
The 21st birthday of Prince Leopold commemorated at Osborne House
and Windsor. At Osborne, band of 102nd (Royal Madras) Fusiliers played
on terrace during luncheon.
Burton-on-Trent. A new church, gift of Mr Bass MP consecreted by Bishop
of Lichfield. Church, parsonage, schools and endowments involved outlay
of approximately £50,000.
Meeting of Monmouthshire and South Wales Colliery Association (Owners)
resolved to support owners of collieries, if necessary from a strike fund.
Price of coal falling and immediate reduction of wages considered.
The 5th annual conference of Elementary Teachers recommended
appointment of a Minister of Education and the selection of inspectors
of schools from among trained teachers.

Death at Munich of Wilhelm von Kaulbach, German painter, (born in Westphalia, 1805)
Birth in London of Sir Nigel Playfair, actor manager,(died August 19, 1934)

Wednesday April 8
Re-opening of Worcester Cathedral, having been in control of architects for 20 years. Repairs etc cost £100,000. Festivities in the town.
Darlington. Foundation stone laid of chapel of a cemetery given by Messrs Pease, owners of mining properties in Durham and Cleveland. Cemetery given in accordance with wishes of their father the late Mr Joseph Pease . . . . . 'so that the working classes should not be compelled to make internments at such great distance, entailing heavy costs and inconveniences.'
The 50th birthday of King of Denmark.
True bill returned by Grand Jury against Carl Lundgren, alias Jean Luie for perjury and bigamy, and against 'Captain' Brown for perjury in connection with the recent Tichborne Case.
Adelaide, Australia. Strike of 2,500 copper miners because of reduction in wages.

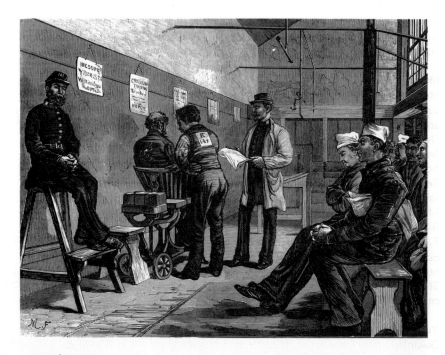

42   *Weighing prisoners at the Clerkenwell 'house of correction'.*

Thursday April 9
Starcross, nr Exeter. Foundation stone of Western Counties Idiot Asylum
laid by Lady Anna Maria Courtenay.
Wigan. Royal Albert Edward Infirmary and Dispensary opened by Earl
of Crawford and Balcarres.
Prince Bismarck ill; visited by Emperor.
Death of Lady Coleridge, mother of Lord Coleridge, aged 87.

Friday April 10
London perjury cases. Jean Luie convicted and sentenced to penal
servitude for seven years, 'Captain' Brown sentenced to five years.
All-England Iron Trade Wages Committee agreed to a reduction of 1s per
ton to puddlers and 10 per cent to well men for three months.
Death of the Marquis of Clanricarde KP. Lord-Lieutenant of Galway,
aged 72.

Saturday April 11
Conference at Mansion House presided over by Lord Mayor of London;
object to organize Saturday Hospital collection in London workshops and
factories.
Peace effective strength of German army fixed at 401,659 men for a term
of seven years ending on December 31, 1881.

Sunday April 12
Queen at Osborne visited by Duke and Duchess of Edinburgh who came by
HM Yacht *Alberta*. Royal salutes fired by warships in Solent.

Monday April 13
Mansion House. Bengal Famine Executive Committee met. Amount
subscribed to date about £80,000. Further sums collected in Manchester
and Liverpool raised total to approximately £100,000.
Dundee. Deputation of Women, mostly wives of leading citizens,
waited on magistrates to urge necessity of reducing number of public
houses in town. Petition signed by 8,303 women.
Severe gales round coasts April 13 and 14. Lifeboats out at Newquay,
saved crew of 20 from *Gutenberg* of Hamburg. Thorpe and Southwold
lifeboats saved 12 and pilot from Alma (Norway) stranded on Sizewell
Bank. Clovelly boat landed crew of four from ketch *Minnie* (Bideford).
Fishguard lifeboat brought in 15 from two schooners.
Survivors of French Transatlantic Steamship Co's steamer Europe, 379 in
number, landed at New York by SS *Greece*.
Stockton, Darlington, Middlesborough and other miners accepted 10 per
cent reduction in wages.

Tuesday April 14
Dukinfield near Manchester. Disaster at Ashley deep pit where 52 killed,
including one rescuer.

Liverpool. Vessel *Glad Tidings* driven ashore near Tralee, all aboard drowned, except one sailor.
Duchess of Teck gave birth to a son.
Sussex with 400 emigrants sailed from West India Docks for New Zealand.
Birth at Kensington of Alexander Augustus Cambridge, Earl of Athlone (died April 14, 1957)

Wednesday April 15
Dr Livingstone's remains landed at Southampton and brought to London.
Body received at rooms of Royal Geographical Society. Reredos in Exeter Cathedral declared to be illegal.
Canada. Finance minister estimated year's deficit of £3 million. Proposed increase in certain taxes.
Death of Lord Kinsale, Irish Peer, aged 46.

Thursday April 16
Louis Riel, Canadian rebel and agitator (1844-85) expelled from Canadian Parliament as a fugitive from justice.

Friday April 17
Alexandra Palace. Cornice carrying part of a wall and scaffolding gave way. One man killed, eight injured, four severely.
Deputation to Home Secretary by Charity Organisation Society representatives, Lord Shaftesbury, Sir Sidney Waterlow and others to point out deplorable condition of working class housing in London. Mr Cross promised 'attentive consideration'.
Adoption of the Military Bill by the German Parliament (See April 11).
Discovery of a new comet by M Coggia at Marseilles (observed and described in Illustrated London News. August 1, 1874).

Saturday April 18
Queen visited Royal Victoria Hospital at Netley, crossing from Osborne by yacht. Streets of Cowes decorated; band and guards of honour in attendance.
Funeral of Dr David Livingstone in Westminster Abbey.
High tide predicted. Great consternation and preparations among Londoners living near Thames banks. (Prediction not fulfilled owing to change of wind).
Birth at San Francisco of Charles Hungerford Mackay, American businessman. (died 1938).

Sunday April 19
Revised Swiss Federal Constitution adopted by people by 280,000 votes against 141,880.
Death of Sir Andrew Orr Kt, Lord Provost of Glasgow, 1854-7, aged 72.
Death of Owen Jones architect and artist, aged 65.

A study of the time, of opera singer Madame Adelina Patti.

Monday April 20
Portsmouth. Duke of Edinburgh laid foundation stone of new buildings for Royal Seamen and Marines' Orphan Schools.
Reduction of 2s per ton of coals on the London market.
Last of men of Hausa tribe from Ashanti expedition arrived at Lagos.
Lieut John Jumbo and remainder of Bonny contingent received at Bonny with all honours.
Severe flooding in Louisiana owing to crevasses in banks of Mississippi; 11 cotton and 14 sugar parishes submerged, destroying 250,000 acres of cotton, 100,000 acres of corn and 500,000 acres of sugar.

Tuesday April 21
County Meeting, Ipswich, presided over by Lord Stradbroke. Resolutions adopted for forming an Agricultural Labourers' Benefit Society.
Annual Spring Agricultural Show of Royal Dublin Society — 'one of the largest ever held'.

Wednesday April 22
Fitzroy Square. Demonstration of lip-reading by deaf children.
About 100 children deaf from birth followed and repeated 'motions of the lips'
Oakham, Rutland. Railway accident — 12-50 passenger train from Leicester ran into by a train being shunted. Several passengers injured.
Death of Lord Thurlow, aged 37.

Thursday April 23
Queen left Osborne House for Claremont House, Esher, and on way inspected at Gosport the Naval Brigade which had taken part in the Ashanti War.

Friday April 24
Mr John Magee, British Vice-Consul at San Jose de Guatemala, received 200 lashes by order of Colonel Gonzales, the commandant who threatened him with execution. Saved by arrival of government troops; Commandant wounded in attempt to escape to an American steamer.
Extensive inundations in consequence of overflow of Mississippi, spreading.
Death of Professor John Phillips MA, LI D, DCL, FRS, geologist, aged 74.
Birth at New York of John Russell Pope, American architect (died 1937).

Saturday April 25
Prince of Wales returned to Sandringham from town. Tyrolese Singers under Herr Helaus sang in evening at Sandringham before Prince, Princess and a large party of visitors.
Preliminary to reopening of Alexandra Palace, a private view given of section intended to illustrate dwellings and domestic dress of all nations. Among exhibits were a modern Egyptian villa and a Moorish residence.
Emigrant ship *Somersetshire* ran aground on Plymouth breakwater in fog. 300 passengers aboard.
Birth of Johannes Stark, German physicist.
Guglielmo Marconi, discoverer of wireless telegraphy born near Bologna, Italy, (died 1937).

Sunday April 26
Annual distribution of prizes of Borough Jewish School held at Lecture Hall, Carlisle Street, Walworth. President Baron Henry de Worms. School contained 65 boys and 52 girls.

German Parliament closed by Emperor in person.

Monday April 27
Queen left Claremont House, Esher, for Windsor Castle.
Royal Geographical Society. Extracts from Dr Livingstone's papers read.
Sir Bartle Frere expressed hope that a connected narrative of his work
might be possible.
The 136th anniversary of Royal Society of Musicians at Willis's Rooms.
Upwards of £1,000 received in subscriptions and donations. Splendid
concert grand pianoforte lent gratuitously by Messrs Broadwood.
Birth in Mayfair, London of Maurice Baring, author (died Dec 14, 1945).
Birth at Finchley of Harry Gabriel Pelissier, entertainer and principal
of 'Follies' concert party (died September 15, 1913).

Tuesday April 28
Prime Minister had audience of the Queen
Mr E Hutchinson, Secretary to Church Missionary Society, accompanied
by Jacob Wainwright, Dr Livingstone's attendant, had audience of Queen.
'The Queen expressed the great interest she felt in the boy'.
Birth of Karl Kraus. Austrian critic and poet.

Wednesday April 29
Grand Ball at Mansion House in honour of marriage of Duke and Duchess
of Edinburgh. Company of more than 1,000 present.
Marquis of Ripon installed as Grand Master of English Freemasons at
Grand Lodge in Temple, Great Queen Street. He appointed Lord
Caernarvon his deputy for the ensuing year.
The 45th anniversary meeting of the Zoological Society, Hanover Square.

Thursday April 30
Dinner party at Windsor Castle. Sir Bartle Frere presented Dr Livingstone's
sons, Thomsas Steele Livingstone and William Orwell Livingstone, to the
Queen.
Bank rate raised from 3½ to 4 percent
Consols, highest price, 93 1/8, lowest 91¾
Emigration returns for the first four months of 1874: 36 ships to US
with 12,354 passengers, 6 to Canada with 2,097 passengers, 2 to Nova
Scotia with 502; 3 to Australia with 108; 5 to United States with 346; 10
to other places with 176. 5,000 labourers, mostly from Dorset and
surrounding countries left England in April owing to lock-out. Emigrants
from Ireland from January to April totalled 22,429.

may

Friday May 1
The 24th birthday of Prince Arthur. Band of 1st Life Guards serenaded under his windows in the morning. Royal salutes.
British Museum closed, to reopen on 8th.
Rev Charles Haddon Spurgeon presided at Baptist Young Men's Association meeting in Metropolitan Tabernacle.
Deputation of friends of Dr Livingstone waited on Lord Derby urging that some provision be made for his family since he had spent some £11,000 of his own money on his explorations.
Levee held by Prince of Wales on command of Queen. Knights of several orders appeared in collars, it being 'collar day'.
Serious disturbances at Ling in Austria because of rise in price of beer, 10,000 people involved. Damage to windows and doors. Machinery, barrels and furniture thrown into Danube. Riot ceased when price was reduced.
Relief of Bilbao by Spanish forces under Marshals Serrano and Concha who compelled Carlists to abandon their entrenchments.
Death of Niccolo Tommaseo, Italian critic and litterateur, aged 71.
Birth at St Leonards of W Lionel Hichens, Chairman of Cammell Laird, business man and public servant (died October 14, 1940).

Saturday May 2
Royal Humane Society. Duke of Edinburgh presided at 100th anniversary festival dinner at Freemason's Tavern. Emperor Alexander, grand-uncle of the Duchess of Edinburgh was one of the first to receive the Royal Humane Society's medal for rescuing a man from drowning.
Woolwich. About 300 gentlemen saw the first portion of the Direct
United New Hampshire Cable placed on board *SS Faraday.* Total length

A distinguished visitor to London was Alexander II, Czar of Russia.

of cable when laid to be 3,060 miles.

Sunday May 3
Total of 23 cottages, a farm house and barns, forming nearly the whole
of the village of Radwinter in Essex, destroyed by fire.
Berlin. Arrival of Czar, with Grand Dukes Constantine and Alexis.
Madrid. Attempted assassination of Senor Pi y Margall by an insane
parish priest who committed suicide.

Monday May 4
Queen, with Princess Beatrice left Windsor by train for London.
Mansion House Indian Famine fund £90,000.Contributions from the
whole of Great Britain estimated at £150,000.

Sheffield. First public park ever opened by Mayor. To be called Weston Park — 12 acres and a large mansion.
Floods in US. New Orleans and Nashville, Tennessee affected. 50,000 rations a day distributed in Louisiana. Flood fund set up in Boston and elsewhere.

Tuesday May 5
Sir Garnet Wolseley entertained at banquet by United Service Club. Prince of Wales, Duke of Cambridge and Prince Christian present.
Czar left Berlin for Stuttgart.
Opening of the Brazilian Chambers by the Emperor.
Death of Marc Gabriel Gleyre, French painter, (born at Chevilly, Canton of Vaud, Switzerland, May 2, 1806)

Wednesday May 6
Queen left Buckingham Palace to return to Windsor.
Price of coal raised 6s per ton on the Coal Exchange.
London. Clothworkers' Company conferred freedom and livery of Company on Sir Garnet Wolseley. Ceremony followed by banquet in Cloth-workers' Hall, Mincing Lane.
Mule and Donkey Show at Crystal Palace.

Thursday May 7
British Museum reopened. Admission to the public Mondays, Wednesdays, Fridays and Saturdays.
Heavy floods still extending in basin of Mississippi and tributaries. Hundreds of square miles swept by rapid currents.

Friday May 8
Emperor of Germany left Berlin for Wiesbaden.
Marriage of Duke Eugene of Wurtemberg with Grand Duchess Wjera at Stuttgart.
Greek Chambers dissolved. New elections ordered for July 1.

Saturday May 9
Queen visited ex-Empress Eugenie at Chislehurst and inspected tomb of ex-Emperor Napoleon III.
Opening of Chelsea portion of Thames Embankment by Duke and Duchess of Edinburgh.
Birth in London of Howard Carter, archaeologist and discoverer of tomb of Tutankhamun, (died March 2, 1939).
Birth of Lilian Baylis, actor manager Old Vic (died November 25 1937).

Sunday May 10
Queen attended divine service in private chapel, Windsor Castle, Rev Francis Holland officiating.
English Church of St Andrew in Corinth, Greece, dedicated by Rt Rev C W

Sandford, D D, Bishop of Gibraltar.

Monday May 11
Exhibition of works of Owen-Jones (died April 19) at 16, Carlton House
Terrace.
Opening of International Flower Show, Florence, by King Victor Emmanuel
II. 300 botanists from all parts of the world present.
Annual distribution of prizes, Ragged Schools Union. Sir W Carden in Chair.
Over 600 young people from 64 schools in London and suburbs 'now in
service' received prizes.
Meeting of Royal Geographical Society. Sir Garnet Wolseley, Sir John Glover
and others spoke on Gold Coast questions and the Ashanti War.
Celebration at Amsterdam of 25th anniversary of accession of King of
Holland.
Birth in London of George Grossmith the Younger, actor manager and
playwright (died June 6 1935).

Tuesday May 12
The University of London resolved to admit women to degrees.
Slave Trade. Meeting at Stafford House presided over by Duke of Teck to
consider question of East African Trade. Speeches by Sir Bartle Frere, Sir
John Glover, Dr Moffat and Mr H M Stanley.
Portsmouth. Banquet for Sir Garnet Wolseley and 100 officers who had
been engaged in Ashanti War, presided over by Mayor.
Czar of Russia embarked on his yacht Derjava at Flushing bound for
Gravesend.

Wednesday May 13
Landing of Emperor of Russia at Dover. Failed to reach Gravesend owing
to delay through ship running on a mudbank in Scheldt. Met by squadron of
ironclads, arrived later at Windsor Castle.
Prince of Wales arrived at Windsor Castle.
Birthday of Pope Pius IX (born May 13, 1792). Congratulations from
cardinals and numerous personages. No disturbances.
Intense heat in New York. Thermometer rose to 90 degrees in the shade.

Thursday May 14
Grand state banquet at Windsor Castle in honour of Czar.
Sir Moses Montefiore Bart admitted to freedom of Fishmongers Company and
presented with a golden casket of address.
Spain. General Dorregaray appointed to succeed General Elio as commander
of Carlist forces in North of Spain.
Famine in Anatolia (Asia Minor).

Friday May 15
Czar received Diplomatic Body at Buckingham Palace.
Marshal Concha appointed to command Republican army in North of Spain.　　**51**

State ball at Buckingham Palace in honour of the Emperor of Russia.

Athens. Judges rejected demand of Turkish Government for half the treasure discovered by Dr Schliemann at Hissarlik and taken to Athens.

Saturday May 16
Queen presented medals to non-commissioned officers who had distinguished themselves in the Ashanti War.

Visit of Emperor of Russia to ex-Empress Eugenie at Chislehurst, to the Houses of Parliament, Westminster Abbey and the Crystal Palace.

Bengal Famine Fund. Mansion House Fund reached £100,000, £80,000 already sent.

Floating Swimming Bath Company's first bath (180 feet by 31 feet) launched at works of Thames Iron and Shipbuilding Company. To be stationed at landing pier, Hungerford Bridge.

Defeat and resignation of the Duc de Broglie's Ministry at Paris.

USA. A large reservoir near Haydenville, Massachusetts, 100 miles north-west of Boston, burst, sweeping away portions of Haydenville, Leeds, Skinnerville and Williamsburg and killing 200 people.

Sunday May 17
Prince Imperial received by Emperor of Russia at Buckingham Palace.
W G Grace (from Australia) with his team and with Dr Livingstone's servants Chuma and Sisi arrived at Southampton on board the *Khedive*.
Death of Sir Roger Therry, formerly judge of Supreme Court, New South Wales, born 1800.

Monday May 18
Reception of Emperor of Russia by the Corporation of London at the Guildhall and presentation of an address.
Strand, London. A man named Colcombe amused himself while waiting to see the Emperor of Russia by pelting people below with paste, from an upper window. He spoiled the cloak of a lady and was subsequently fined 45s.
Algiers. A train arrived late from Oran, delay caused through rails being covered by 'a thick layer of grasshoppers'.
Constantinople. About 100 houses in suburb of Galata destroyed by fire.

Tuesday May 19
Review at Aldershot in presence of Emperor of Russia.
State Ball at Buckingham Palace.
Opening of City Temple on Holborn Viaduct, London. Pastor Joseph Parker DD, Lord Mayor of London and Sheriffs attended.
Birth at Cheltenham of Gilbert Jessop, famous cricketer (died May 11 1955).

Wednesday May 20
Queen left Windsor Castle at 8 pm for Balmoral, arriving Thursday.
Emperor of Russia visited Woolwich Arsenal.
Close of farm labourers' dispute in Lincolnshire.
Evening banquet in Merchant Taylors Hall, on occasion of 220th anniversary festival of the Sons of the Clergy. Service in St Paul's. Total contribution and legacies £5,663.
Annual Concert of Tonic Solfa Association. Crystal Palace; programme consisted of pieces illustrating The Seasons.

Thursday May 21
Embarkation of Emperor of Russia from Gravesend on departure from England.
A deputation waited on Bishops of Gloucester and Bristol to present a memorial signed by more than 900 people as a protest against ritualism.
St Mark's Church, Victoria Park, London. Ceremony to acknowledge presentation of a chiming clock and peal of bells to mark the Queen's satisfaction with her visit in 1873 to the East End. 'During the day the bells played several airs'.
Meeting of British Anti-Slavery Society addressed by Sir T Fowell Buxton on prevalence of slavery in Africa, Fiji Islands and elsewhere.

Close of sessions of both houses of Prussian Diet.

Friday May 22
Statue of Sir James Outram unveiled in Calcutta by Lord Napier.
Emperor of Russia disembarked at Flushing, and arrived Brussels.
Close of Swedish Diet by King Oscar.
Birth at West Cowes, IOW, of Sir Cyril T M Fuller, admiral (died February 1
1942).
Birth in Cape Colony, of Daniel F Malan, future Prime Minister of South
Africa (died February 7 1959).

Saturday May 23
New baths and lecture hall opened by London Swimming Club. Named
Crown Baths, situated at rear of Oval.
Prince Hohenlohe, new German Ambassador, received in Paris by Marshal
MacMahon, President.
Loss of HM ship *Niobe,* a 5-gun sloop at Cape Blanc, Miquelon.
Completion of submarine telegraphic cable between Constantinople and
Odessa.
Death of Sylvain van de Weyer, formerly Belgian Minister in London, age
72. His death 'caused Her Majesty profound grief. He had been for many
years one of the Queen's most valued friends.'

Departure of the Emperor of Russia in his yacht from Gravesend.

Close of sessions of both houses of Prussian Diet.

Friday

Sunday May 24
The Queen's 55th birthday. On this day the Queen elevated Prince Arthur
to the peerage with titles of Earl of Sussex and Duke of Connaught and
Strathearn.
Princess Louis of Hesse gave birth to a daughter.

Monday May 25
Whit Monday. Holiday arrangements completely spoiled by heavy thunder-
storms. Return trains crowded with half-drowned excursionists only too
glad to get home. Fine in evening for fireworks. Museums, National Gallery
and Brighton Aquarium crowded.
Execution of James Godwin in Newgate for the murder of his wife.
King Victor Emmanuel of Italy refused to accept resignation of Signor
Minghetti, the Prime Minister.
Count Claudio Faina of Orvieto, returning from a fair at Viterbo, captured
by brigands; £8,000 put on his head, and finally murdered.

Tuesday May 26
Prince Arthur gazetted as Duke of Connaught and Strathearn and Earl of
Sussex.
'Festival for children' at St Katherine Cree, London. Congregation of
young people, most of whom carried flowers. The Rector spoke on the
virtues of the common plant.
Barnstaple. Devon County Agricultural Show opened.

Wednesday May 27
First meeting of Four-in-Hand Club held at Magazine in Hyde Park. Duke
of Beaufort, President of Club, led off the procession.
Paisley. Townspeople had general holiday to celebrate centenary of birth
of Robert Tannahill, held by them to be Scotland's greatest poet and song-
writer after Burns.

Thursday May 28
Queen present at funeral of Peter Farquharson, 'one of Her Majesty's
oldest servants who faithfully discharged the duties of Keeper for 27 years.'
Bank rate reduced from 4 to 3½ per cent.

Friday May 29
Servants celebrated at Balmoral in honour of Queen's birthday.
Consols. Highest price 93 3/8, lowest 92¾.
The new Swiss Constitution came into force.
Emperor and Crown Prince of Germany visited Prince Bismarck.
Death of Jean Louis Hamon, French painter at St Raphael (born at
Plouha, May 5, 1821).
Birth at Campden Hill, London, of Gilbert K Chesterton. English author
and humorist, (died June 14 1936).

Saturday May 30
Her Majesty's birthday celebrated. Prince of Wales represented Queen at guard-mounting at the Horse Guards in celebration.
Bayswater. Baths and wash-houses opened at Queens Road by Lord Mayor.
Great display by largest gathering of volunteers held in Hyde Park, Regents Park, Wimbledon and elsewhere.
United States 'Decoration Day' when friends of soldiers who had fallen in the Civil War visited graves and took flowers.

Sunday May 31
Dublin. Roman Catholic University dedicated by Cardinal Cullen to the Sacred Heart of Jesus.
Birth at Belgrave Square, London, of Giles S H Fox-Strangways, Earl of Ilchester, historian, (died October 29 1959).

june

Monday June 1
Ashanti War Exhibition visited by the uncle of King Coffee Calcallee,
the only Ashanti to be met in Europe. 'This gentleman is an Englishman
and Christian by education, is named Prince John Ansah or Ossoo Ansah,
son of King Osai Tootoo Quamina (died in 1826)' (*Illustrated London
News*).
Tramway line opened to Southall, Tooting and Shepherds Bush.
New railway line from Sevenoaks to Maidstone opened. Maidstone wore
a holiday aspect.
Joseph Arch presided over the executive meeting of the Agricultural
Labourers' Union. A move to settle disputes by arbitration, but not at the
sacrifice of wages. Over 2,000 still reported locked out — an increase of
more than 200.

Tuesday June 2
London. Site of Church of St Martin Outwich, more than 2,200 sq ft, sold
by Ecclesiastical Commissioners to Messrs Hardwick and Holmes, solicitors,
for £32,000.
Cambridgeshire and Huntingdonshire. Severe thunderstorms. Boy with three
horses returning from ploughing, killed at Kimbolton.

Wednesday June 3
Derby at Epsom won by *George Frederick* with *Couronne de Fer* second.
The 9th birthday of Prince George, second son of the Prince of Wales (later
King Geroge V).
Lord Mayor entertained provincial mayors at banquet, Mansion House.

Thursday June 4
Bank rate reduced from 3½ to 3 per cent.
St Paul's. Annual sermon to charity school children preached by Bishop
Carlisle. Service attended by Lord Mayor, Sheriffs and Common
Councillors.
Moscow. Great fire, 57 residences in 3 streets destroyed, damage estimated
at 500,000 roubles.

Friday June 5
The Oaks, at Sevenoaks, won by *Apology*
Willis's Rooms, London. The 4th Annual Meeting of Christian Evidence
Society. Bishop of London in Chair. Question of infidelity considered.
Others present — Archbishop of York, Bishops of Gloucester and Bristol.

Saturday June 6
London. Firm in Minories summoned for copying trade name 'Yorkshire
Relish' with a forged and counterfeit trade mark. Defendants tò insert an
apology in newspapers, surrender all counterfeit labels and pay fine of £5.
'Hockey on Horseback'. Opening of new polo ground of the Hurlingham
Club.
Hastings. Dispute about rights of Corporation to seashore, raised through
defendant making excavations and carting soil away — settled in favour
of Corporation.
Florence. Monument to late Prince Rayaram of Kolapore, who had died
there in 1870, publicly unveiled.

Sunday June 7
Her Majesty attended divine service at Crathie Church, Rev A Campbell
of Crathie officiating.
Death at Basle of Karl Rudolf Hagenbach, German church historian
(born Basle, March 4, 1801).
Birth at St Helens, Lancs of Sir Rigby P D Swift, Judge died October
19 1937.

Monday June 8
Prince Arthur took his seat in Lords as Duke of Connaught.
Blackburn. Bishop of Manchester denounced all vested interests in pews as
being opposed to theory of a national church.
Opening of Bath and West of England Agricultural Show, Bristol.
United States. Letter published in newspapers from Foreign Minister of
Guatemala to Her Majesty's Charge d'Affaires expressing sorrow at the
deplorable affair of the flogging of Mr John Magee, promising punishment
and reporting an offer of £10,000 compensation. (See April 24)

Tuesday June 9
St Pancras. Conference of delegates from Metropolitan vestries on price
of gas.

Aston Hall Colliery. Mr Gladstone addressed miners on question of unionist intimidation.

Rome. Pope received about 2,000 American pilgrims. Valuable presents offered to His Holiness.

Wednesday June 10
State Concert given by Her Majesty at Buckingham Palace. Prince and Princess of Wales with members of Royal Family present. Artistes included Mme Adelina Patti, Mr Charles Santley, the Italian Opera, Philharmonic and Sacred Harmonic Societies.

Bedford. Statue of John Bunyan unveiled by Lady Augusta Stanley.

London. Lord Mayor's Banquet to Her Majesty's Judges, the magistracy and the bar.

Thursday June 11
Covent Garden Theatre. Production of Michael William Balfe's posthumous opera 'Il Talismano.'

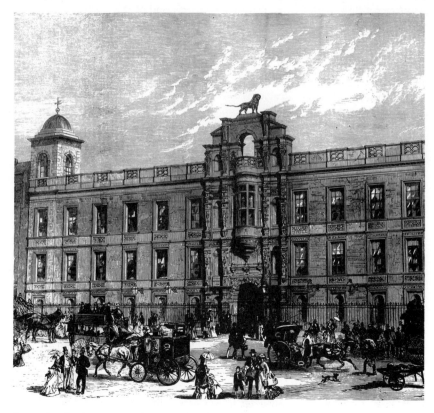

Scene in the Strand outside Northumberland House.

German State Council voted extension to all Germany of the new Prussian law for registration of births, deaths and marriages.
San Francisco. Two sharp earthquake shocks felt. No damage or casualties.

Friday June 12
Concert of blind performers, singers and pianists given by pupils of Royal Normal College and Academy of Music for the Blind.
Venice. Opening of Roman Catholic Congress.

Saturday June 13
London. 'Grand Day' at Middle Temple when Prince of Wales dined with Benchers.
London. Woman convicted of robbing children of articles of clothing in the street. Imprisoned for three months.
Paris. Louis Henri Renouard charged with an assault on statesman M Leon Gambetta with a stick. Declared that he intended to provoke M Gambetta to a duel. Imprisoned for six months and fined 200 francs.

Sunday June 14
Hospital Sunday. Collections amounted to £29,300.
Grand Prix of Paris won by English horse *Trent.*
Death of Sir Charles Fox, builder of Crystal Palace in 1851 (born 1810).

Monday June 15
Line from Bournemouth to Poole opened by Somerset and Dorset Railway.
Brisbane, Queensland. Victoria Bridge opened (commenced 1864).
Civil Marriage Bill rejected by German Federal Council.
Resignation of Danish Ministry.
Paris. Motion by M Casimir Perier in favour of a formal recognition of the Republic in France, carried in French Assembly by 345 votes against 341. Opposition mainly monarchists and bonapartists.

Tuesday June 16
Leicester. The 40th annual conference of British Temperance League.
British Museum visited by 45 Eton boys with their masters.
Ascot Stakes won by Lord Lonsdale's *Coventry.*
Arrival of Henri Rochefort at Queenstown where he was mobbed (see March 31).

Wednesday June 17
London. Opening at Society of Arts Rooms of International Conference on the prevention of cruelty to animals. Presided over by Lord Harrowby. Most European countries represented.
London. Lord Mayor's Banquet to archbishops, bishops and clergy.

Thursday June 18
Bank rate reduced from 3 to 2½ per cent.

Ascot Gold Cup won by M Delamarre's *Boiard.*
The 32nd annual meeting of Field Lane Ragged School supporters. Lord
Shaftesbury in chair, 1,000 present.
Rome. Celebration of 28th anniversary of accession of Pius IX.
King of Holland arrived at Ems. Received at station by Emperors of Russia
and Germany.

Friday June 19
Ascot. Alexandra Plate won by *King Lud.* Ascot Plate won by *Lowlands.*
Crystal Palace. Handel Festival commenced. Conductor Sir Michael Costa
(Festival ended on the 26th).
Turkish vessel *Kars,* en route for Salonica, run down in Sea of Marmora.
Only 30 saved out of total of 350 passengers and crew.
Death at Passy, near Paris of M Jules Gabriel Janin, French critic (born
St Etienne, Loire, February 16, 1804).
Death at Shayok in Ladakh of Ferdinand Stoliczka, Austrian
palaeontologist (born Hochwald, Moravia, May, 1838).

Saturday June 20
The 37th anniversary of the accession of Queen Victoria.
Manchester. Great trades demonstration in support of locked-out
agricultural labourers.
Cleveland miners' strike terminated with acceptance of employers' terms.
Wooden bridge over River Don between Mexborough and Denaby
destroyed by fire.
Engagement in Sumatra between Dutch and Achinese, the latter driven
back from banks of River Achin with great loss.
Death of Sir J R Wolseley, cousin of Sir Garnet Wolseley (born June 24
1834).

Sunday June 21
First anniversary of opening of St Saviour's Church, Oxford Street,
exclusively for the deaf and dumb. Anniversary service in sign language.
Bishop of London preached to a mixed congregation including Lord
Shaftesbury and other distinguished persons. Words of speakers interpreted
to deaf and dumb in sign language.
Rome. Brilliant reception to celebrate Papal anniversary (June 16, 1846).

Monday June 22
Demonstration of about 20,000 miners at Willenhall on open space
among pits. Strong feeling for continuing struggle 'to the bitter end.'
Mr Plimsoll at Eastern Hall, Limehouse in connection with London Seamen's
Mutual Protection Society.
Royal Geographical Society, meeting at London University, Burlington
Gardens. Sisi and James Chuma, Livingstone's servants presented with
bronze medal by Sir Bartle Frere. (See May 17).
South Africa. Bishop Colenso appealed to the Governor in Council on

Ladies of fashion at Henley Regatta.

behalf of the rebel chief Langabalele.
Bengal Famine Relief (Mansion House) Fund reached £117,023.
Telegraphic communication established between Europe and Brazil.
Paris. Funeral of Jules Janin (see June 19) attended by 3,000 persons including the whole of the Paris literary and artistic world.

Tuesday June 23
Queen left Balmoral for Windsor, arriving Wednesday at 9 am.
Alhambra Music Hall, Bristol, destroyed by fire.
London. Lord Shaftesbury presided at public meeting in St George's Hall on behalf of Committee of Plimsoll Seamen's Fund.

Close of the session of the United States Congress. President Grant
signed 'Poland Act' providing for prosecution under criminal law by
US Attorney-General for cases of polygamy. (NB The Act was not well
administered and was only one step in its eventual abolition).
Syracuse, New York State. During a festival the floor of a church gave
way. Four killed, more than 100 injured.

Wednesday June 24
State ball at Buckingham Palace by command of the Queen.
Freedom of Merchant Taylors Company conferred on Mr Disraeli and
the Marquis of Salisbury.
Henley Regatta spoilt by violent thunderstorms. Royal Thames Yacht
Club race for Queen's Cup won by the *Kriemhilde.*
Severe thunderstorms everywhere. Woman struck dead sitting by her fire
at Mossymouth Toll, five miles from Elgin. Free Church at Ardoch in
Perthshire struck. Men killed in Fifeshire.
Nuremberg. National commemoration in honour of Hans Sachs (1494-
1576), people's poet. Unveiling of statue.

Thursday June 25
Arrival of Crown Prince and Princess of Germany at Spithead.
More severe thunderstorms in Scotland. Flooding at Newburgh, Fifeshire.
Fruit crops badly damaged.
Berlin. Suspension of German Working Men's Association.

Friday June 26
Archbishop of Canterbury presided over annual meeting of National
Society for Promoting the Education of the Poor. Willis's Rooms, London.
Protest against legislation obstructing liberty of religious teaching and
disadvantages under which denominational elementary schools were
placed financially.
Rome. Pope received members of Roman nobility who had remained
faithful to the Holy See, informing them that in spite of requests made to
him to leave Rome 'we have remained and shall remain as long as God
and circumstances will permit.'
Shock of earthquake felt at Constantinople.

Saturday June 27
Pupils of Royal Normal Schools and Musical Academy for the Blind,
Upper Norwood, played and sang for Her Majesty at St George's Hall.
Officers presented to Queen.
Farningham. Annual Summer Fete for Home for Little Boys. Prizes
distributed by W E Forster MP.
Brussels. King of Belgium opened Agricultural Exhibition.
Death in action of Marshal Manuel Gutierres de Concha while attacking
Carlist entrenchments at Muro. Marshal Concha was a veteran of the
Spanish War against Napoleon.

Birth at Elswick, Newcastle-on-Tyne of Henry J F Badeley, Baron;
Clerk of Parliaments (died September 27, 1951).

Sunday June 28
The 36th anniversary of coronation of Queen Victoria, who attended divine
service in Royal Memorial Chapel, Frogmore and received Holy Communion.
Paris. Grand review of troops by Marshal MacMahon.

Monday June 29
Annual Benefit Concert at Royal Albert Hall for Mr Sime Reeves.
Messrs Ashdown and Parry of Hanover Square bought copyright of late
Signor Guglielmo's song 'The Lover and the Bird' for £716.
General Zabala appointed to succeed Marshal Concha as commander of the
army in the north of Spain.

Tuesday June 30
Inter-university cricket match won by Oxford.
Essex Agricultural Association annual exhibition at West Ham Park.
Westminster. Earl of Shaftesbury presented prizes for window gardens of
the labouring classes in College Gardens.
Westminster. First of a series of statues to be placed in Park Square — a
full-size bronze figure of the late Lord Derby — hoisted on to its pedestal.
Captain Schmidt, a German war correspondent, captured on the 25th,
shot by Carlists at Estella.

july

Wednesday July 1
Buckingham Palace. State concert attended by Prince and Princess of Wales.
Bedford. A deputation of locked-out agricultural labourers assembled and began their march through the provinces.
Farewell dinner to Mr J L Toole, comedian, preparatory to his departure for America.
Vienna. Count Andrassy opened International Sanitary Conference, object to devise measures to prevent spread of cholera.
Birth in London of Sir Nigel Playfair, actor-manager (died August 19, 1934).

Thursday July 2
Leicester Square. New garden handed over by Mr Albert Grant to the Metropolitan Board of Works. Total cost had been £28,000. Now 'made pleasant and beautiful.' Shakespeare statue by Fontana. Address of thanks from Leicester Square Defence Committee.
Burlington House. Annual Reunion of President and Council of the Royal Society of Arts.

Friday July 3
Drawing-room meeting at 36 Kensington Gardens to raise £10,000 for premises for a Mission Home for Young Englishwomen in Paris (founded 1872).
Crown Prince and Princess of Germany arrived on Isle of Wight.
Comte de Chambord issued manifesto to French people.
Spain. An Englishman, Arthur Haselden captured in Linares district by brigands.

The new gardens in Leicester Square, London.

Saturday July 4
Independence Day in United States. General holiday.
Miners on strike at Cannock Chase agreed to accept masters' terms and
resume work.
Great bridge across Mississippi at St Louis opened. Cost 9 million dollars.
London. Deputation of Fiji Aborigines Protection Society and well-known
colonists waited on Lord Caernarvon with memorial in favour of annexation
of Fiji Islands.

Sunday July 5
Queen, Princess Beatrice, Prince Leopold attended divine service in private
chapel at Windsor Castle, officiated by Rev Edward Wickham, Headmaster
of Wellington College. In evening, dined with Duke and Duchess de
Rochefoucauld Bisaccia at French Embassy.
King of Holland and King of Belgium both arrived at Ostend.

Monday July 6
Opening of 15th meeting of National Rifle Association, Wimbledon.
For the first time paper-covered targets superseded iron targets.
Women's Suffrage meeting at Westminster Palace Hotel. Speakers,
Frances Power Cobbe, Mrs MacLaren, Miss I Tod.
Dover. Deep water basin opened by Lord Granville, Lord Warden of

Cinque Ports and President of Dover Harbour Board.
Emperor of Germany left Weimar for Coblenz. Emperor of Russia
arrived Weimar from Jugenheim.
Death of Lord Dalhousie (born April 22, 1801)..

Tuesday July 7
Germany. Horses drawing Empress of Russia and King of Saxony through
streets of Dresden took fright. No injuries.
Emperor of Russia left Weimar for Warsaw.
British Museum. Address by George Smith to the Society of Biblical
Archaeology on the recent excavations at Nineveh.

Wednesday July 8
Chobham. Review by Queen of troops engaged in summer manoeuvres.
'Tichborne v Tichborne' before Court of Probate. Claimant's declaration
that as Lady Tichborne had died intestate he, as next of kin, was entitled
to property, struck out as no one appeared.
Regents Park. The 3rd annual Evening Fete, 9,000- 10,000 present.
Gardens illuminated with electric light. Duke and Duchess of Teck attended.
Chess. Herr Zuckertort, blindfolded, conducted ten games simultaneously
against strong amateurs of the City of London Chess Club without seeing
either the boards or the men. Games adjourned until Friday.

Thursday July 9
Queen's Dinner Party at Windsor Castle. Prince and Princess of Wales and
Crown Prince and Princess of Germany present.
Death of Vincent de Groof, 'the flying-man' by falling with his newly-
invented parachute from a balloon which had ascended from Cremorne
Gardens. Parachute made in imitation of bat's wings. Balloon descended
in Essex in front of an oncoming train which stopped just in time.
Wimbledon rifle meeting. Lords defeated Commons by 76 points.
Corporal Young, 1st Herts, won silver medal and £20 prize for second
time.
Cable-laying steamer *Faraday* arrived at Portsmouth, New Hampshire
after having been delayed by fog. (See May 2).

Friday July 10
Crown Prince and Princess of Germany arrived London. Met by Prince
and Princess of Wales.
Highgate. Lady Burdett Coutts distributed prizes for encouragement of
gardening among the poor, and rewards to persons pledging themselves to
protect wild birds, their nests and eggs.
Chess. Herr Zuckertort won 5 games, drew 4 and lost one. (See July 8).

Saturday July 11
Crown Prince and Princess of Germany visited Royal Academy.
Heavy thunderstorms in London. Many houses flooded.

Memorial statue of Lord Derby in Parliament Square unveiled by
Mr Disraeli. (See June 30).
Italy. Bread riots reported in Pisa.
United States. Cheyenne, Comanche and Kiowa Indians, able to muster
3,000 men, threatening war. Attacks feared on settlements.
Chicago. Opening of a Chinese theatre, cost $50,000. First performance,
to an audience of 3,000, lasted from 7 pm to 3 am.
USA. Inter-collegiate Boat Race at Saratoga between Columbia, Wesleyan,
Harvard and Yale. Columbia 1st, Harvard 2nd.

Sunday July 12
Emperor of Germany, arriving from Mainau at Salzburg, on visit to Emperor
and Empress of Austria.
Crown Prince and Princess of Germany went to divine service at Westminster
Abbey.

Monday July 13
Visit of Crown Prince and Princess of Germany to opening of Royal
Agricultural Society's show at Bedford.
Aquatic entertainment by London Swimming Club in Serpentine.
Bradford. Ceremonial opening of St James's wholesale fish, fruit and
vegetable market. Cost — £13,000.
Ulster. Orange demonstrations to celebrate July 12 near Belfast. 100,000
persons estimated to be present. 'The proceedings appear to have passed off
quietly.'
Attempted assasination of Prince Bismarck at Kissingen in Bavaria by a
youth named Kullmann, a member of the Catholic Young Men's Society.
Emperor of Russia arrived at Tsarskoe Selo.
Arthur Haselden released by Spanish brigands on payment by his friends
of £6,000 (see July 3).

Tuesday July 14
Queen left Windsor Castle for Osborne House. Duke of Edinburgh
arrived at Dover from Continent.
Private Atkinson, 1st Durham Rifle Volunteers, won Queen's Prize at
Wimbledon.
Pentonville. Clergy of St Philip's promoted show of window boxes,
plants and industrial work.
E W Pugin, architect, tried at Criminal Court for having libelled Mr J R
Herbert R A. Acquitted on ground that his letters, though scurrilous,
were not libellous. (See June 2).
Emperor of Russia arrived at St Petersburg.
Formation of a new Danish Ministry under presidency of M Fonnesbeck.

Wednesday July 15
Crown Prince and Princess of Germany attended Polo match at Royal
Horse Guards and Polo Club.

Glasgow. Property worth £30,000 to £40,000 destroyed by the bursting of the banks of a canal.
Constantinople. Great fire in Galata quarter destroying 200 houses and causing £200,000 damage.

Thursday July 16
Crown Prince and Princess of Germany at Aldershot Sham Fight and luncheon at mess of 7th Hussars.
Sir Bartle Frere presented with freedom of City of London.

Friday July 17
Duke of Edinburgh, after visiting Queen, left for Darmstadt to meet Duchess.
Crown Prince of Germany visited Archbishop of Canterbury at Lambeth Palace and inspected Palace.
Children of Fitzroy Ragged School taken in vans to Roebuck Inn, Buckhurst Hill, for a dinner of roast beef and plum pudding.
Bicentenary of Isaac Watts (born July 17, 1674) celebrated by noncomformists of his native town, Southampton.
Postal convention between France and the United States ratified at Washington.

Thames sailing-barge matches.

Saturday July 18

Surrey v Middlesex match. 'Surrey have obtained 30 years' lease of the Oval at a very low cost.'

Wigan. Ince Hall Coal and Canal Co pit disaster. Fifteen men killed by explosion in one pit, 19 lives lost altogether.

The 500th anniversary of death of Italian poet Petrarch celebrated at Padua, at Avignon and at Arqua where he died. Crowds of tourists at Avignon. Address given by Senor Quintana, a Spaniard who called on Latin races to unite against 'pure Germanism'.

India. Business at Bombay at a standstill owing to excessive rains.

Sunday July 19

Crown Prince of Germany inspected St Thomas's Hospital and German Hospital.

The whole of Spain declared in a state of siege and a levy of 120,000 men ordered.

Monday July 20

Crown Prince of Germany left London for Portsmouth and Spithead. Inspected ironclads *Friedrich Karl* and *Ariadne.*

Northumberland House, Charing Cross, due for demolition, open to the public all this week.

West Ham Park opened as a public recreation ground.

Opening of new railway line connecting Ilfracombe and Barnstaple. Illuminations and beacon fires on hills.

Emigrant ship *Eastern Monarch* completed voyage from Plymouth to Canterbury, New Zealand in 71 days 19 hours from land to land, and from port to port in 73 days 12 hours (May 7 - July 20). 'One of the fastest passages ever made by a sailing vessel.'

Tuesday July 21

Marriage of Marquis of Waterford with Lady Blanche Somerset, only daughter of the Duke of Beaufort.

Lord Mayor of London gave a banquet at the Mansion House to 300 ladies and gentlemen, representatives of literature, art, music and the drama. Present were Mme Patti, Lord Lyttelton, Sir George Elvey, Sir Julius Benedict, Mr G A Sala, Sir Francis Gaunt (President of the Royal Academy), Sir Arthur Helps and others.

Great heat and heavy thunderstorms in Midlands and North; some deaths from sunstroke and lightning.

Ryde, IOW. Victoria Yacht Club gave a banquet to Crown Prince and Princess of Germany at the Club House.

Wednesday July 22

Marlborough House. Prince and Princess of Wales gave a fancy dress ball. Over 500 royal and distinguished personages present.

Mansion House. Lord Mayor's Banquet. Mr Disraeli and most of the

Making ice.

chief members of the government present.
Azagra, Portugal. Disastrous landslip; village destroyed; 200 bodies taken
from ruins.

Thursday July 23
Princess Charlotte of Prussia attended by Count and Countess Eulenberg
left Marlborough House for Sandown.

Friday July 24
Camborne, Cornwall. Opening of Wesleyan Methodist Conference.
Empress Eugenie and Prince Imperial, making tour of continent, visited
Grand Duke and Duchess of Baden on island of Mainan on Lake
Constance.

Saturday July 25
Over 10,000 Forest of Dean miners held 3rd annual demonstration.
Mr Halliday announced that Staffordshire strike had cost the miners
£50,000.
Experiment in 'aerostation.' A balloon equipped with steering apparatus,
invented by Mr Bowdler, ascended at Woolwich. Apparatus failed to guide
the balloon as intended and could only make it rise and revolve right or
left.

Sunday July 26
Crown Prince of Germany arrived at Blenheim Palace on a visit to Duke and
Duchess of Marlborough.
Hughenden, Bucks. Service performed for the last time in the church
standing in the park of Mr Disraeli's residence before extensive restoration.
Consecration of Roman Catholic Cathedral at Dublin. Twenty Papal bishops
present including five from England.
Earthquake shock felt in Vienna.

Monday July 27
National Agricultural Labourers' Union declared that it could not support
strike any longer and recommended labourers to emigrate. The strike had
cost £25,000 out of union funds.
Bellot Strait, North-west Territory, Canada. Captain Kilgour of whaler
Poynia discovered records left in a tin canister by Capt William Kennedy of
the *Prince Albert,* a vessel searching in 1852 for the expedition of Sir John
Franklin, lost in 1845.
Disastrous floods in Pennsylvania causing appalling loss of life.
Death of Baron Anselm Rothschild in Vienna, age 72.
Death of John H Foley RA, eminent sculptor (born Dublin 1818).
Remains interred in St Paul's Cathedral.

Tuesday July 28
Successful experiments on Metropolitan Railway with self-acting foul air
exhaust and vacuum brake, allowing driver to have control over the whole
train.
Leamington. Midland Counties Croquet Tournament. Fifteen entries for
Leamington Champion Prize. Total prize value — £50.
Inverness. Opening of Highland Society's Agricultural Show.
Caithness railway line opened.
Liverpool. Landing stage on Mersey destroyed by fire.
American floods extended to Ohio and Kentucky; 219 lives lost in
Pittsburgh alone.
Outrages of Indians increasing. More troops needed to cope with Cheyennes.

Wednesday July 29
Empress Elizabeth of Austria, travelling incognito, left Vienna en route for
Isle of Wight.
King of Denmark arrived at Reykjavik for 1,000th anniversary of colonisation
of Iceland.

Thursday July 30
Bank rate raised from 2½ to 3 per cent.
Consols, highest price 92¾, lowest 92⅜.
Married Women's Property Act passed. Extent of liability of a husband for
his wife's debts limited.

Friday July 31

Dr Frankland FRS declared water supplied to London by New River Company to the metropolis slightly turbid and containing living organisms.

Coping stone of western arch of Temple Bar sank several inches. Cause believed to have been the digging of foundations for the new Law Courts.

Death of Thomas Carrick, famous miniature painter at Newcastle-on-Tyne. Age 72.

Death at Bromley, Kent, of Charles Tilstone Beke, traveller, geographer and biblical critic (born Stepney, October 10, 1800).

august

Saturday August 1
Queen drove to Sandown and visited Crown Prince and Princess of Germany.
Empress of Austria arrived at Ryde from le Havre and went to Steephill
Castle, Ventnor, specially prepared for her.
Rt Hon Andrew Lusk MP, Lord Mayor of London, created a baronet.
Statue of Dr Joseph Priestley unveiled at Birmingham on centenary of day
on which he discovered oxygen. Address given at Town Hall by Professor
Huxley.
Statue of Sir Titus Salt unveiled at Bradford by Duke of Devonshire.

Sunday August 2
Death of Rt Hon, Sir George James Perceval, 6th Lord of Egmont and 3rd
Baron Arden.

Monday August 3
Bank Holiday weather fine. A crowd of 36,489 visisted Crystal Palace,
11,740 visited Brighton Aquarium, 9,207 visited International Exhibition
at South Kensington.
Working Men's Club and Institution Union's 6th annual excursion to
Duke of Westminister's splendid estate of Cliveden Park near Maidenhead.
Over 2,000 took part.
Leicester. Mayor laid, with masonic honours, memorial stone of new
Municipal buildings, estimated cost £30,000.

Tuesday August 4
Spain. Eleven of the gang of brigands who had seized Mr Haselden (see
July 3) sent for trial to a criminal court.
Germany. Bishop Conrad Martin arrested at Paderborn. Sentenced to 18
weeks imprisonment.

Wednesday August 5
Close of the session of French Assembly.
Ministerial whitebait dinner at Greenwich.
Birth at Roslin, Midlothian of Sir William Paterson, mechanical engineer
(died August 9, 1956).

Thursday August 6
Bank rate raised from 3 to 4 percent.
King of Denmark formally welcomed at Icelandic celebrations.

Friday August 7
Prorogation of Parliament till Friday October 23.
Agricultural labourers on the march carrying collecting boxes taken into
custody at Bradford.

Saturday August 8
Cowes week began. Prince and Princess of Wales present. They 'made
various cruises and witnessed several regattas'.
Emperor of Germany arrived at Berlin after visiting Gastein.

Sunday August 9
Marshall Bazaine, escaped from confinement on the Island of St Marguerite
during the night of the 9th - 10th (See December 25, 1873)

Monday August 10
The 35th anniversary meeting of Royal Botanical Society, Regents
Park. Exhibition of flowers etc.
Excursions by members of Epping Forest Fund Committee to Monk Wood

The China tea-ship Glenartney.   75

near Loughton — partly enjoyment and partly to assert right of public to use the property.

Dunmow. Effort to revive Dunmow Flitch ceremony, first since 1869. Flitch awarded to Mr Clegg, age 38, a clerk in the office of the Standard Measure Wine Company in St Mary Axe, living in Brixton, and his wife — 'one of the worst trials ever staged.'

Death of Sir James Walsham, Bart, (born 1805).

Birth at West Branch, Iowa of Herbert C Hoover, American President 1928-32, died New York, October 20, 1964.

Tuesday August 11

Pope received 100,000 francs sent by one of the Catholic Associations of London.

Madagascar. H M *Vulture* (commander A T Brooke), cruising off north-west coast, gave chase to a slave ship. When boarded, 41 men, 59 women and 137 children found in a terrible condition. The owners were 35 armed Arabs. *Vulture* burned the dhow and sailed for Seychelles.

Wednesday August 12

Grouse shooting began.

Liverpool. A band of agricultural labourers left this month for Canada on SS *Dominion*

Relief of Derry celebrated by procession of Apprentice Boys and Orangemen in that city.

Thursday August 13

Plymouth. Prince of Wales opened new Guildhall and Law Courts.

Crown Prince and Princess of Germany at Isle of Wight Horticultural Society Flower Show.

Death of Hon Sir James Lindsay KCMG (born August 25, 1815)

Friday August 14

Crown Prince of Germany presented new colours to 106th (British Regiment).

Cardiff colliery owners decided to reduce wages by 10 per cent on and after September 1.

Gold Coast Colony. Terrific fire in native town of Bonny. Most crowded half of town destroyed.

Birth at Tottenham of John K Fotheringham, historian and author of books on ancient astronomy (died December 12, 1936).

Saturday August 15

In Durham 30,000 miners assembled for 4th annual demonstration.

Glasgow. Monster Home Rule demonstration held. Between 30,000 and 40,000 took part.

The American game of baseball exhibited at Lords Cricket Ground by players of the Philadelphia Athletic Club.

A fine sketch of the new Guildhall, Plymouth, opened in August 1874 by the Prince of Wales.

Town of Liakhovitchky in Government of Minsk, destroyed by fire; 329 houses, a church, a presbytery and 3 synagogues lost. Two women died.
Birth at Morges, Switzerland of Dame Evelyn E M Fox, pioneer mental health worker (died June 1, 1955).

Sunday August 16
Archbishop Manning gave a temperance address to some 500 persons assembled on Tower Hill. At conclusion about 400 men, 50 women and some children signed pledge.

Monday August 17
Crown Prince and Princess of Germany laid foundation stone of new Ryde School of Art, then visited Queen at Osborne.
Strike of Leicestershire miners began against pay reduction of 6d a day.

Tuesday August 18
Wigan. Miners in mass meeting refused to accept owners' recommendation of a reduction in wages of 15 per cent.
Bangor. Welsh National Eisteddfod inaugurated.
Marshall MacMahon continued his tour of France, visiting Le Mans and Leval.
Death of Sir William Fairbairn, Bart, of Ardwick, Manchester, engineer and

coadjutor of George and Robert Stephenson (born February 19, 1789, at Kelso, Roxburghshire).

Wednesday August 19
Opening of 44th annual meeting of British Association at Belfast.
Professor Tyndall delivered opening address as President.
Brussels. Dinner given in King's Palace in honour of the Duchess of Edinburgh.
Birth at Moseley, Birmingham of Arthur R Buller, botanist and mycologist (died July 3, 1944).

Thursday August 20
Queen left Osborne for Balmoral
Bank Rate reduced from 4 to 3½ per cent
Typhoon at Nagasaki, Japan
Birth at Salford, Lancs, of Benjamin O Purse, blind social worker and expert in blind welfare (died March 31, 1950).

Friday August 21
Queen arrived at Balmoral.
Bow Street. Summons withdrawn against Mr Purcell, *Westminster Gazette,* for printing an alleged libel in an article written by Mr E Welby Pugin on Mr Herbert, RA. Pugin committed for trial for writing the libel.
Coal-owners of Newcastle proposed reducing Durham miners' wages by 20 per cent. Decision adjourned for one week.

78   *The dramatic scene at the burning of the landing stage at Liverpool docks.*

Saturday August 22
Skipton. Fifteen persons charged for stoning vicar of a church who had disputed payment of a grave-digger's fee. Five fined, rest discharged.
Demonstration at Swanscombe, Kent of workmen in protest against suppression of cement factories near Northfleet.
Total of 336 emigrants sailed for South Australia on assisted passages. These included 66 single women domestic servants 'greatly wanted in the colony.'
Jarrow. Richardson's paper mills destroyed by fire. Damage £30,000 to £40,000.
Lima, Peru. Attempt by band of assassins on life of President Pardo.
Death of Sydney Thompson Dobell, poet, (born April 5 1824 at Cranbrook, Kent).

Sunday August 23
Princess of Wales, accompanying her father the King of Denmark, arrived at Copenhagen.
Sneinton, Nottingham. Cotton factory of Mr S Morley MP burnt down. £100,000 damage. Some suspicion of incendiarism.

Monday August 24
Prince of Wales left Osborne and went to Promenade Concert at Covent Garden.
Consecration of Archdeacon William Basil Jones as Bishop of St David's.
Leamington. Executive Council of Agricultural Labourers' Union met; £170 voted for emigration purposes.
Hanley. Explosion at Abberley Colliery. Four men out of five in pit died.
After discovering new land and wintering among ice floes, Austrian polar expedition reached Puchewa Bay and contacted a Russian schooner.

Tuesday August 25
Prince of Wales left Marlborough House for Potsdam to be present at confirmation of eldest son of Crown Prince and Princess of Germany (later Emperor William II).
At Princes Club, Manchester, Mr Herbert Barge shot a Mr Maclean dead and then committed suicide.
Emperor of Russia reviewed Baltic Fleet at Cronstadt.

Wednesday August 26
Birthday of Prince Consort. Tenants and servants at Balmoral drank to the memory of His Royal Highness at the Obelisk.
Liverpool. A second band of 500 agricultural labourers left for Canada accompanied by Mr Henry Taylor, Secretary of the National Union on board the *Dominion.* The Secretary intended to stay for some time to ascertain living conditions of recent emigrants.
Branch of Severn and Wye Railway opened from Cinderford Valley, Dean Forest via Lydbrook to Ross and Monmouth.

Tourists halt at a country inn for a leisurely drink.

Formation of a new Dutch Ministry at the Hague.

Thursday August 27
Bank rate reduced from 3½ to 3 per cent
Clackmannan miners voted to reject owners' terms.
Deputation to Sir E Watkin MP and Directors of South Eastern Railway
Co, to protest against threatened discontinuation of workmen's trains in
South and South-east London suburbs.
USA. Cheyennes, Kiowas and Comanches in force on warpath and making
a raid on Texas.

Friday August 28
Duke and Duchess of Edinburgh travelled from London to Balmoral.
Lord Mayor and Lady Mayoress of London also there.
Great Western Railway half-yearly meeting. Sir Daniel Gooch MP
expressed regret at the 'obnoxious impost' which the Government still
persisted in laying on third-class passengers.
St Petersburg. Marriage of Grand Duke Vladimir with Duchess Marie of
Mecklenburg.

Saturday August 29

A patient at Manchester Infirmary died of hydrophobia from the bite of a dog, received in February last.

Southend. Artillerymen from Shoeburyness called out to aid police in dealing with roughs who had carried off a barrel of oysters and assaulted fishermen.

Birkenhead. Launching of new ironclad turret ship *El Plata* built by Messrs Laird for Argentine Confederation.

6,000 Fife and Clackmannan miners locked out.

Nottingham. Mr S Morley advised work-people of Sneinton to find work elsewhere as he could not employ more than a few. He was paying all his employees one-third wages for the time being (see August 23).

Wandsworth. For putting his arm round a barmaid's waist and kissing her, a butcher was sentenced by a magistrate to pay a fine of 30s and costs.

Eruption of Mount Etna.

Prince of Wales, with Crown Prince of Germany, paid a visit to Emperor and Empress.

District Council of Lower Alsace adopted a resolution asking for a separate constitution and diet.

Sunday August 30

Mons Kubecazag, appointed Archdeacon of Xions for his friendly disposition towards the Prussian government, celebrated his first service. 'It would appear that his appointment has not given satisfaction to the peasants, a large body of whom broke into the church and assaulted him.' Troops called in.

Monday August 31

Consols, highest price 92 7/8, lowest, 92 3/8.

South Lancashire miners refused to accept reduction in wages and asked for arbitration.

Merthyr Tydfil. South Wales miners accepted terms offered by employers — 10 per cent reduction — by majority of 20,000.

Aberdeen tramways, laid on more than three miles of streets, opened for traffic.

Bournemouth. Spa Hotel opened 'in the picturesque suburb of Boscombe.'

M Duruof, a French aeronaut, started from Calais in a balloon with his wife to cross straits to Dover, but was carried out to sea.

Paris. Last stone of Vendôme column laid and tricolor placed on summit.

Birth at Williamsburg, Mass, of Edward Lee Thorndike, American psychologist, (died August 9 1939).

september

Tuesday September 1
Blackburn, Lancs. Greater part of town flooded by torrential rain.
Annual Show of East Cheshire Agricultural Society opened.
Hull. State yacht of Cesarewitch launched and named *Czarevna*.
Nearly 400 pilgrims set off from London for religious services at shrine
of St Edmund at Abbey Church of Pontigny, 118 miles south-east of
Paris.
New railway line from Halifax to Ovenden (part of Halifax-Bradford
line) opened to traffic.
The aeronaut Duruof and his wife picked up at sea by fishing vessel near
Dogger Bank. Balloon made off towards Norway.

Wednesday September 2
Marquis of Ripon resinged Grand Mastership of Freemasons of England,
he having joined the Roman Catholic communion.
Meeting of inhabitants of High Holborn to protest against shortening
of its name to Holborn.
North and East Yorkshire, afternoon. Tremendous thunderstorm, the
worst since 1866, two known fatalities.
Pilgrims to Pontigny met there by Archbishop Manning.
Berlin. Review of Guards on anniversary of Battle of Sedan (September 1-2,
1870) Prince of Wales, in uniform of Coldstream Guards, rode on right
of Emperor.

Thursday September 3
Bolton, Lancs. Cotton spinners resolved to resist 5 per cent reduction in
wages by strike action if necessary.
Arrival of Austrian polar expedition at Vardö island, Norway, on return

journey.

Earthquake in Guatemala, loss of 200 lives.

Death at Lemnitz, Sax Weimar of Hans Conon von der Gabelentz, German linguist and ethnologist (born Altenburg, October 13, 1807)

Friday September 4

Meeting of N and NE Lancs cotton spinners who resolved, in view of trade conditions, to ask members to put their employees on short time – a 4 day week, beginning October 1.

Funeral of J H Foley R A eminent sculptor, in St Paul's.

Apology made to British flag in San Jose de Guatemala, in consequence of outrage on British consul (See April 24)

Rio de Janeiro. Celebration of anniversary of Brazilian independence.

Anniversary of fall of French Second Empire (1870). Disturbances by bonapartists at Perigueux, Agen and Meze (Herault)

Saturday September 5

Rates of mortality for the week

Bristol	17	Sunderland	26	Bradford	29
Portsmouth	17	Manchester	27	Sheffield	29
London	19	Hull	27	Salford	30
Norwich	19	Birmingham	28	Newcastle	32
Oldham	22	Leeds	29	Wolverhampton	32
Nottingham	26	Leicester	29	Liverpool	32

Latest available figures for other cities.

Paris	21	Christiania		Rome	25
Brussels	23	(Oslo)	21	Turin	19
The Hague	18	Berlin	38	New York	36
Amsterdam	24	Breslau	36	Philadelphia	23
Copenhagen	30	Munich	32	Madrid	37
		Vienna	20		

Aberdeen. Duke of Edinburgh laid foundation stone of a new breakwater.

Notice of 20 per cent reduction served on 40,000 Durham miners.

Sunday September 6

Meiningen, Germany. Great fire. Half the town reduced to ashes and more than 3,000 people rendered homeless.

Monday September 7

Northampton. A balloon ascent could not be effected because of insufficient gas. An irritated crowd tried to set balloon on fire and, failing to do so, tore it to pieces.

Emperor Francis Joseph of Austria arrived at Prague. Enthusiastic reception.

Tuesday September 8

Empress of Austria visited Ventnor athletic sports. Earl of Dudley presented her with a thoroughbred worth upwards of 600 guineas.

Brighton. New church of St Bartholomew, Anne Street, opened. Cost £16,000.

Teddington. Boat designed by Mr H M Stanley, for Central African Expedition, launched at yard of Mr Messenger and named the *Livingstone*.

London. Meeting of City Commission of Sewers reported that since July 28, 16 tons 6 cwt of diseased meat had been seized at London markets and slaughterhouses, and the Fishmongers Co had seized and destroyed since August 8th 112 tons of fish unfit for human food.

Jersey. Election of the Jurat. Party feeling found vent in several hostile encounters in the streets.

Amsterdam. Great fire. Extensive sugar factory, insured for 1,500,000 florins, destroyed.

Wednesday September 9

London. Opening of new line on Metropolitan and District Railway from Earls Court to Hammersmith.

Blackwall. 500 emigrants left East India Docks — mainly agricultural labourers from home counties — bound for Queensland.

Reading. A platform gave way at a performance of Sanger's Circus. Several persons badly cut about the face and hands.

St Neot's, Huntingdonshire. A fierce storm broke down sheds at Huntingdonshire Agricultural Show. Liberated animals careered fiercely across the showyard. Nobody injured.

Thursday September 10

Rail disaster at Thorpe, near Norwich, 28 killed and many injured.

Millwall. New Brazilian ironclad *Independencia* launched at Messrs Dudgeon's Yard.

Fire at premises of Raphael and Co, commission agents, Bishopsgate Street, London. £40,000 damage.

Friday September 11

Brecon. Opening of Brecknockshire Agricultural Show.

Capt Strahan sworn in a s Governor of the Gold Coast and the new Charter read.

Emperor William of Germany left Berlin for Hesse.

Geneva. Congress of International Law Association ended.

Saturday September 12

Poplar..Ironclad *Deutschland* constructed for German Government, launched from yard of Samuda Bros.

Bow Street. A middle-aged and shabbily dressed man giving name of Albert Saxon and describing himself as 'the most sensible man in all England' charged with being a lunatic at large. He believed he was the

Extricating the dead and wounded at a railway disaster at Thorpe, Norwich.

Queen's first born and was soon to be installed as Prince of Wales.
Greenford. Miss Anne Dodd bound over to keep the peace and fined
£5 for attacking a tax-gatherer with a knife.
Emperor William of Germany present at review of troops before the
Grand Duke of Hesse. Prince of Wales present.
Death of Francis Pierre Guillaume Guizot, eminent French statesman and
historian (born October 4, 1787 at Nîmes).

Sunday September 13
Queen, Duke and Duchess of Edinburgh and Princess Beatrice attended
Divine Service at Crathie Church. Rev Dr MacGregor of St Cuthbert's
Church, Edinburgh officiated.
Princess of Wales and her children at Copenhagen. Prince, travelling
under title of Earl of Chester, on way from Baden to join his family.
Re-opening of church-ship on Tyne *Diamond* with a service. Ship well
known as Sir William Paul's old frigate in Crimean campaign.
France. Elections in Department of Maine-et-Loire. Republicans headed

poll with 45,359 against Septennist (Orleans) 26,093 and Bonapartist 25,570. A second poll required.
Birth at Vienna of Arnold Schoenberg, Austrian composer. Died July 13, 1951.

Monday September 14
Royal Institution, Albemarle Street. First meeting of Congress of Orientalists under presidency of Dr Birch of British Museum.
M Duruof, famous balloonist, ascended from Crystal Palace, landing at Ingatestone, Essex. M and Mme Duruof's stray balloon (see August 31 and September 1) landed at Hull after being picked up by a fishing smack 250 miles from Humber and 100 from Norwegian coast.
Young Men's Christian Association (founded 1844) National Conference at Bristol.
Gaolers of Ile Ste Marguerite appeared before tribune of Grasse accused of assisting in escape of Marshal Bazaine from island. (See July 9).

Tuesday September 15
Blenheim Park. Annual meeting of Woodstock Agricultural Association.
Berne, Switzerland. Meeting of International Postal Congress.

Wednesday September 16
First show of North Cardiganshire Agricultural Society opened. More than 600 entries.
Southport. New Winter Garden and aquarium opened. Eight acres, lawns, promenades, fountains, a band pavilion etc. Cost £100,000.
Glasgow. Meeting of public bodies to consider best means of purifying the Clyde.
Berne. International Postal Congress decided to move for a uniform system of postal charges for all countries.

Thursday September 17
Prince of Wales arrived at Copenhagen aboard royal yacht *Osborne.*
Inverness. Great Assembly of aristocracy of North Scotland, instituted in 1788 and since observed without interruption, took place (ending 18th). Brilliant gathering in full Highland costume, Highland dancing and games. Thousands present at spectacle.
Empress of Austria inspected Royal National Hospital for Consumption at Ventnor, Isle of Wight.
Christiania (Oslo), Norway. Arrival of members of Austrian Arctic Expedition.
France. Trial ended of Marshal Bazaine's gaolers. Two warders imprisoned for six months, one for two months, one for one month. Marshal's valet and two gaolers acquitted.

Friday September 18
Aberdeen. Fungus exhibition, 7,000 specimens contributed 'by almost

every fungologist in Britain.' Several species new to science exhibited.

Saturday September 19
Mansion House. International Congress of Orientalists ended with banquet given by Lord Mayor of London.
Contradictory reports being circulated about health of Arthur Orton (Tichborne Case). Lord Rivers, who had seen him in prison stated that he was in good health though he had lost 7 or 8 stone in weight.
Bow Street. Carl Johann Södenberg, a Swede, charged with being a lunatic at large. He believed that the Dowager Queen of Sweden owed him a fabulous sum of money for discovering a silver mine. Committed to a workhouse pending repatriation.
Opening of legislative chambers of Netherlands by the King.
Kiel. Launch of the German ironclad *Friedrich der Grosse* in presence of Emperor of Germany who had arrived from Hanover.
Death of Louis Huard, famous Belgian artist, aged 60.

Sunday September 20
Pope received members of Roman nobility faithful to his cause who brought an address deploring 'the occupation of the Eternal City, the greatest dishonour of the civilised savages of an ungrateful Europe.'
Rome. Monument bearing the names of the men killed in the taking of Rome (September 20, 1870) unveiled.

Monday September 21
Clerkenwell. Meeting to promote a movement in favour of free opening of the Tower of London.
Bedworth Colliery, North Warwickshire. Numbers of men refused to go down the pit after hearing nocturnal sounds, probably made by migrating birds, but believed by them to be The Seven Whistlers to whom they attributed several recent accidents.
Dutch Parliament opened by King who commented on progress made in the work of draining the Zuyder Zee and expressed hopes of ending the war in the East Indies.
Death of Jean Baptiste Armand Louis Leonce Elie de Beaumont, French geologist (born Canon in Calvados, September 25, 1798).
Birth at Cheltenham, of Gustav Holst, English musician and composer (died May 25, 1934).

Tuesday September 22
London. Meeting of City Commission of Sewers to consider widening of Fleet Street in neighbourhood of Temple Bar, to range the buildings in line with Law Courts then being erected.
Aberdeen. Town Council resolved to vote freedom of City to Mr Disraeli.
Grand review of garrison of Copenhagen in honour of the Prince of Wales.
Hong Kong (night). Typhoon of unprecedented violence swept island.
Loss of life estimated at 1,000. Five ships sunk, six missing, two ashore,

three dismasted. Immence amount of property destroyed. In all 24 English and American vessels reported as casualties.
Typhoon also swept South Japan and Macao. Heavy loss of life. Between 2,000 and 5,000 lives (total not known) lost. About 600 Chinese vessels sunk.
Birth of Sir Ernest Barker, scholar (died February 17, 1950).

Wednesday September 23
USA. Military forces sent to Alabama owing to disturbances between negroes and whites there.

Thursday September 24
Empress of Austria, travelling incognito under title of Countess Hohenembs, arrived at Steephill Castle, Ventnor from London.
E Welby Pugin's trial for libel on Herbert continued. Ordered to enter on his own recognisances for £500 and 2 securities of £250 and come up for judgement when called upon.

Friday September 25
Unveiling of statue of composer Michael William Balfe in Drury Lane Theatre. Limehouse. Two lifeboats for Russia paid for by St Petersburg residents as marriage present to Duke and Duchess of Edinburgh, to be called the *Alfred* and *Marie* tested and launched at docks of Messrs Forrest.
Vienna. Members of Austrian Arctic expedition enthusiastically received by people.

Saturday September 26
New York. International rifle match between England and America won by

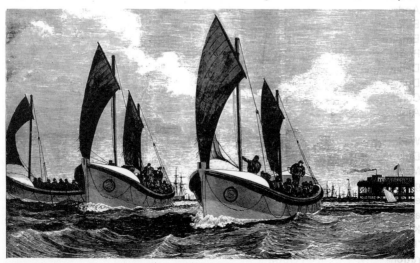

Scene during the life-boat race at Deal regatta.

America, by 9 points on 1st range and 3 points on 2nd.
French elections Maine et Loire, second round. Republican nominee 51,515
votes. Septennists' nominee 47,728.
By death of Thomas Thurlow (a nephew of the late Lord Chancellor) on
April 22, 1874, Government ceased to pay a pension of nearly £12,000 a
year received on account of abolition of various offices.

Sunday September 27
Dublin. Cardinal Cullen announced in a pastoral letter that he regarded a
scene in Balfe's opera *Il Talismano* a burlesque on Catholic religious
ceremonies. (Prohibition of Catholics to visit theatre later brought about a
modification of this scene).
Milan. Victor Emmanuel II, King of Italy visited Exhibition of Industrial
Art. Congratulated members of municipality on progress of works going on
in the Cathedral Square.
Birth at Balsall Heath, Birmingham, of Sir Robert Howson Pickard, chemist
(died October 18, 1949).

Monday September 28
Duke of Edinburgh visited Liverpool, reviewed artillery and rifle volunteers,
laid foundation stone of new art gallery to be erected by Mayor and
presented to the town.
Steephill Castle, Ventnor. The ex-Queen of Naples visited her sister the
Empress of Austria.
Wiesbaden, Germany. Opening of Protestant Congress.

Tuesday September 29
London. Liverymen met at Guildhall to elect Lord Mayor to succeed Sir
Andrew Lusk. Mr Alderman Stone elected.
Empress of Austria and ex-Queen of Naples visited Ventnor steeplechases.
Empress presented a cup.
Prince and Princess of Wales at a dinner party given by King and Queen of
Denmark at Fredensborg.
Duke of Edinburgh attended musical festival at Philharmonic Hall, Liverpool.
Conductor, Sir Julius Benedict and among performers, Mme Patti, Mme
Albani, Mr Sims Reeves and Mr Charles Santley.

Wednesday September 30
Duke of Edinburgh opened newly-erected Liverpool Seamen's Orphanage.
Marylebone.. A revolver was produced in court following a charge of a
gentleman that his wife had threatened to shoot him with it. While being
examined the revolver, apparently loaded many years previously, went off
and a bullet struck the bench.
King of the Fiji Islands ceded them to the British Government.
'In the year ending this day the Hospice of St Bernard distributed 64,114
rations as well as much clothing to 17,221 poor travellers and 147 invalids.
Many, half-frozen, were cared for by the monks.'

october

Thursday October 1
Close of Duke of Edinburgh's visit to Liverpool.
Departure of Empress of Austria from Isle of Wight after a stay of six weeks.
Prince and Princess of Wales left Copenhagen for Stockholm.
M Thiers had audience of King of Italy at Milan.
Nice. Severe storm. Fourteen fishermen struck by lightning; two killed and
the rest injured.

Friday October 2
Terrific gunpowder explosion on a large barge proceeding down the
Regents Canal, London, under the Avenue Road Bridge. The bridge blown
up by about five tons of gunpowder. A 'colossal disaster' to property
around. At least three dead, many injured and many rendered homeless.
Most damage done to house of M Alma Tadema, Belgian artist.
Manchester. Professor Huxley opened new School of Medicine connected
with Owen's College.

Saturday October 3
Resolution passed at Guildhall, London (President Lord Mayor) to support
Hospital Saturday on 17th instant.
Damascus. Fever raging; 14,000 persons, including half the garrison, attacked.

Sunday October 4
Temple Church, London which had been closed for several weeks, re-opened.
Arrest and imprisonment of Count Arnim, late German Ambassador in Paris,
on a charge of having in his possession state documents.
Guatemala. Complete reparation made for outrage on Consul Magee. British
flag saluted and indemnity of £10,000 paid to him. (See April 24).

Empress of Austria arrived at Baden-Baden after her stay in England.

Monday October 5
Glasgow. Social Science Congress. Dr Lyon Playfair spoke on the comparison of death rates in London (average 21.4) with principal towns (average 26.9), small towns (average 20.2) and rural districts (average 16.2) and conclusions to be drawn.
A little girl living in service at Hillingdon attacked by bloodhounds belonging to her master while cooking food for them and severely mangled.
Copenhagen. Prince and Princess of Wales at opening of Danish Parliament by King.
Egypt. Great alarm caused by extraordinary rising of Nile which reached a height of 26½ cubits (over 40 feet).
A train, passing along a branch line of the Somerset-Dorset railway, ran off the rails, falling off a bridge into a stream dragging tender and guard's van with it but leaving carriages behind. Driver killed, foreman and two officials injured. A few passengers slightly hurt.
Death of Bryan Waller Procter (Barry Cornwall), poet, born at Leeds, November 21, 1787.

Tuesday October 6
Brighton Pavilion. Opening of Anglican Church Congress.
Maidenhead. Important meeting of West Berkshire Agricultural Association. Discussion on level of agricultural wages.
Torquay. Baroness Burdett Coutts distributed prizes to donkey drivers and carters who had distinguished themselves by 'humane treatment of the brutes under their control.'
Southport. Cambridge Hall opened to supplement Town Hall by Rt Hon Assheton Cross, Home Secretary.

Wednesday October 7
Duke of Edinburgh laid the foundation stone of the new wing of the Royal Female Orphan Asylum at Plymouth.
Broussa, Turkey. Turkish soldiers (200) broke into the Armenian Catholic Church, dragged out the Bishop, desecrated sacred vessels and wounded many of the congregation.

Thursday October 8
Great Ormond Street, London. Commencement of the 21st year of the Working Men's College. Subjects taught — English grammar and literature, Latin, Greek, French, German, arithmetic, algebra, geometry, physical geography and geology.
Reading. Foundation stone of new municipal buildings laid.
Hereford. Opening of Free Library by Bishop and wife of the donor, Mrs Rankin.
Queen Dowager of Bavaria received into the Roman Catholic Church.
Birth at Newport, Mon, of James Henry Thomas, labour politician and cabinet minister (died January 21, 1949).

Friday October 9

Tunbridge Wells Agricultural Show opened.

Opening of Hythe and Sandgate branch of South-eastern Railway.

Berne. International Postal Congress. All states represented except France, signed convention.

Archbishop of Cologne released after six months in prison. Further imprisonment remitted in consideration of suspension of salary and sale of his furniture.

Saturday October 10

Exceptionally large number of spots visible on sun, covering area of nearly 78,000 square miles.

Hyde Park. Great open-air meeting in aid of Hospital Saturday Fund, Archbishop Manning in chair. More than 20,000 attended with bands and banners.

USA. Serious situation in Alabama. A White League organised and armed. Political murders committed daily.

Sunday October 11

Prince of Wales left Copenhagen on Royal yacht *Osborne* en route for Paris.

Manchester. Meeting of English Synod of United Presbyterians. 106 congregations and 19,754 members represented.

French cabinet recalled ship *Orénoque* from Rome. This ship had been placed at Pope's disposal should he desire to leave Italy.

Monday October 12

Huddersfield. Conference of Congregational Union of England and Wales opened.

Opening of narrow gauge railway from Plymouth to Exeter by way of Tavistock, Lidford and Okehampton, across Dartmoor.

Town of Akkolyi, Turkey, of 5,000 inhabitants, destroyed by fire.

Senor Avellaneda installed as President of Argentine Republic at Buenos Aires.

Tuesday October 13

Metropolitan Bridges Association meeting. Resolutions passed approving action taken by Metropolitan Board of Works with a view to freeing of Thames bridges of tolls.

Hammersmith. In connection with a case of assault after a wedding, prisoner said his sister was married on Sunday and they had been drunk ever since. The magistrate remarked that an Irish wedding without a broken head was a very extraordinary thing.

Episcopal Synod, Armagh opened, Lord Primate in Chair. He condemned a majority of the Synod who declared for a revision of the Prayer Book.

Wednesday October 14
Opening of Leeds Musical Festival with Mendelssohn's *St Paul*. Conductor, Sir Michael Costa.
Public meeting of parishioners of Whitechapel to consider offer of £12,000 by E O Cooper MP towards the erection of a new church. Committee appointed to raise a further £6,000.
Paris. Prince of Wales called on Marshal MacMahon.
Birth at Staines, of Thomas Ashby, archaeologist (died May 15, 1931).

Thursday October 15
Son born to Duchess of Edinburgh at Buckingham Palace.
Arrival of Empress of Russia and Cesarewitch at Buckingham Palace.
Falmouth. Iron-built ship *Candahar* (1410 tons) arrived with no jib-boom, bowsprit, and leaking. Had collided with *Kingsbridge* (1497 tons) which sank with master, his wife, daughter and eight of the crew. Estimated loss £30,000.
Berlin. Search of Count Arnim's house. Several unopened chests seized. (See October 4).
Springfield, Massachusetts. Monument to late President Lincoln unveiled.

Aventurière winner of the Cesarewitch at Newmarket.

Friday October 16
Wisbech. Joseph Arch, agricultural trade union leader, declared that the labourers had not been defeated in the recent great lock-out. About 900 had left the district and 800 had been taken on again by masters without surrendering their union cards.

Saturday October 17
The first Hospital Saturday in the metropolis. About £4,000 collected.
Visit of the Prince of Wales to the chateau of the Duc de la Rochefoucauld-Bisaccia, late French Ambassador at St James's, at Esclimont, in France.
Indictment of Brigham Young for polygamy. (See US legislation on polygamy June 23).

Sunday October 18
Evening. Grand dinner at Buckingham Palace. Many British and Russian notables met Empress of Russia.
Prince of Wales entertained to dinner by the Duc de la Tremouille at Rambouillet, nr Paris. Menu included tartlets a la Talleyrand, roast beef and potatoes a la Dauphine, capons a la Regence and glaces a l'Orleans.
German parliament opened by Prince Bismarck.

Monday October 19
On and after this day compartments for ladies could be reserved on all trains of the Metropolitan Railway.
Bayswater. Public meeting at Clanricarde College to establish a Society for Natural History and Physical Science. Many prominent scientists present.
Cincinnati. Balloon ascent made by Professor Donaldson accompanied by a bridal party of six persons. When it was about a mile high the marriage ceremony was performed.

Tuesday October 20
Prince Leopold attended his first meeting of the Privy Council.
Parliament prorogued to Wednesday December 16.
Empress of Russia visited Haymarket Theatre accompanied by Cesarewitch and Duke of Edinburgh.
Hastings. New life-saving device consisting of the seats of a boat covered with cork, demonstrated.
East Norfolk Railway (Norwich-North Walsham) opened for traffic.
Death of Karl Gustav Homeyer, German jurist (born August 13, 1795 at Wolgast, Pomerania).

Wednesday October 21
Cesarewitch visited ex-Empress Eugenie at Camden House, Chislehurst.
Severe gales. Iron steamship *Chusan* dashed on rocks at Ardrossan; 15 lost.
Three drowned off Laxey, Isle of Man, three boatmen drowned at Deal, two men thrown into river at Sunderland and drowned. Blickling Hall, Norfolk, in severe gale, damaged by fire.
Birth at Scarborough of Sir T E Cooper, architect (died June 24, 1942).

Thursday October 22
Prince and Princess of Wales left Copenhagen en route for Paris.
Freedom of the City of London presented to Sir Garnet Wolseley.
Liverpool. A woman named Parr brought up in court for not sending her
child to school, produced a note purporting to have come from the child's
teacher — 'to the shool Board I do sertify that Davet Paur Atends my Shool
Every Day Margret Pilkinson.'

Friday October 23
Cyclone in Bay of Bengal; 2,000 lives lost at Midnapore.
Negro riots in Louisiana.
Death of Abraham Geiger, Jewish theologian and orientalist (born
Frankfort-am-Main May 24, 1810).

Saturday October 24
Hertfordshire. Desperate poaching affray. Poachers threw stones and
presented fowling-pieces at keepers. Men on both sides wounded in hand-to-
hand fight in which poachers defeated keepers.

Paris Autumn Fashions.

Sunday October 25

Rome. First English church erected within walls of city — Holy Trinity, Piazza S Silvestro, opened. Congregation 180.

Death of Thomas Miller, author of many popular novels and literary works. Age 66.

Birth at Skipton-in-Craven, Yorks, of Geoffrey Dawson, twice editor of *Times* newspaper (died November 7, 1944).

Birth of Charles F G Masterman, author and journalist, at Spencer Hill, Wimbledon (died November 17, 1927).

Monday October 26

Princess of Wales arrived at Paris.

Shetland. Arrival of the *Camperdown,* a whaler bringing 32 whales and 175 tons of oil, total value nearly £100,000, the most successful catch for many years.

Worcester. The largest public meeting ever held met under presidency of Mayor to protest against action of Dean and Chapter in refusing use of Cathedral for meeting of the Three Choirs in 1875.

Note in *Gazette* confirming award of Victoria Cross on Major Reginald William Sartorius, 6th Bengal Cavalry for valour in the Ashanti War.

Tuesday October 27

Foundation stone of a new market at Billingsgate laid by Mr Rudkin, Chairman of Markets Committee of London Corporation. To contain 39,000 superficial feet as against former market's 20,000.

Over, Cheshire. Fire at Haigh's cotton mill. Nine workpeople burnt to death. Woman and child killed by jumping from a window.

Death of Owen D Young, American politician, lawyer and businessman.

Wednesday October 28

Interview of the Metropolitan Association with the Home Secretary on the subject of a new municipality for London.

Prince and Princess of Wales left Paris for London and arrived later in day at Marlborough House.

Blackwall. Launch of ironclad frigate *Oudiyeh* built by Thames Ironworks for the Sultan of Turkey.

Thursday October 29

Ex-Empress Eugenie visited Prince Imperial at military establishment, Shoebury, Essex.

Consols, highest price 93, lowest 92 ⅜.

Grantham. Foundation stone of new hospital on a site given by Earl Brownlow in Manthorpe Road, laid by Countess Brownlow.

Portsmouth. Foundation stone of new gaol (estimated to cost £40,000) laid. Ceremony followed by a mayoral function.

Cambridge. Ely diocesan conference decided to take steps to raise funds to rebuild North-West Transept of Ely Cathedral. Cost estimated £25,000 to

£28,000.

Friday October 30
Freedom of Rothesay, Scotland, presented to Marquis of Lorne.
Death of Edwin Lankester MD, LID, FRS, eminent doctor, scientist and
coroner for Middlesex, aged 60.

Saturday October 31
End of International Exhibition, Kensington. 'Every class pronounced it a
failure and indeed it was the most depressing of places . . . simply because
the public did not and would not come to it.' (Illustrated London News,
October 31).
Chrysanthemums in the Temple Gardens, London in bloom a full fortnight
before their usual time.
Exeter. Opening of block of 24 model tenements for working people.
Between May and October 16,889 persons reported to have been banished to
Siberia. Of these, 1,220 described as criminals, 1,624 expelled from communities as obnoxious and/or burdensome, 1,080 women and children over 15
and 1,069 young children voluntarily accompanied the exiles.
Birth at Edinburgh, of Sir R Fleming Johnston, scholar, traveller and
administrator (died March 6, 1938).

november

Sunday November 1
Trier (Treves), Alsace. Herr Schneiders, an exiled chaplain, arrested after having celebrated divine service. Attempts to rescue him unsuccessful.

Monday November 2
Balmoral Castle. Picturesque hallowe'en festival in which Queen and Princess Beatrice took part.
London. Alderman Stone, Lord Mayor elect, presented to Lord Chancellor.
RIBA. Sir Gilbert Scott appealed for dispassionate consideration of questions connected with decoration of St Paul's and expressed regret at Mr Ruskin's refusal to accept Gold Medal of the Institute. (See March 9).
Election of town councillors in municipal boroughs of England and Wales.

Tuesday November 3
Visit of Prince and Princess of Wales to Birmingham. Town brilliantly decorated and illuminated.
Meeting at Mansion House of Bengal Famine Fund. Close on £130,000 collected by Lord Mayor's Committee. Balance to be sent to India. Secretary of the Fund to receive a gift of plate worth £100.
Gold Coast. Governor Strahan met kings and chiefs on subject of the buying, selling and pawning of slaves. Read message of Queen concerning abolition of trade. King Coffee reported to have been deposed and gone to the villages beyond Coomassie.

Wednesday November 4
Spain. Bombardment of Irun by Carlists begun.

Thursday November 5
Prince and Princess of Wales at Coventry.
Bristol. A little boy, firing off a pistol, killed a girl standing near him, the
weapon having been loaded with rivets.

Friday November 6
Hammersmith. A boy, one of a mob who had annoyed a man who had married
sooner than was thought proper after the death of his first wife, by 'playing
rough music on kettles and throwing stones', fined 10 shillings.
Birth at Edinburgh, of Catherine Mary Stewart, Duchess of Atholl (died
October 21, 1960).

Saturday November 7
Prince and Princess of Wales returned from Coventry to Marlborough House.
New Lord Mayor of London, Alderman Stone sworn in. At a speech later he
expressed opposition to the projected Bill for the municipal government of
London, thinking that it would in time extinguish the privileges of the
Liverymen.
Meeting of the Directors of Great Northern, Great Western, Lancashire and
Yorkshire, London and North Western and other railway companies.
Resolution passed that the Midland Board be requested to postpone action
regarding the abolition of the second-class and reduction of first-class fares
until after the half-yearly meetings.
Darwen, Lancs. In a violent attack of typhoid fever, 44 deaths had been
reported since October 8.
About 12,000 Durham miners agreed to leave the settlement of their quarrel
to arbitration and the Umpire, the Recorder of London, made an award
reducing their pay by nearly 10 per cent.
Elstree, Boreham Wood. A train parted in the centre, the first running into
a tunnel and becoming fixed, the wheels of a carriage having left the rails.
Two carriages shattered, one person killed and several injured.

Sunday November 8
Leeds. Meeting of shareholders of Midland Railway. Directors urged by
large majority to refrain from altering fares and abolishing second-class until
other companies had been consulted.

Monday November 9
The 33rd birthday of Prince of Wales. Celebrations at Sandringham. Dinner
given to 220 labourers on royal estate.
Annual banquet at Guildhall 'passed off hilariously'. Mr Disraeli, the Prime
Minister played his part 'with customary felicity.'
Eastbourne beach. Beginning of a week's mock siege operations against
batteries thrown up on beach by R E recruits.
Paris. Lieut Zubowitz, of Hungarian Honved Corps, arrived after riding from
Vienna on one horse within 14 days. As he entered Paris on the fifteenth day
he lost the bet he had made.

The Prince and Princess of Wales visit a factory in Birmingham.

Tuesday November 10
Opening meeting of Royal Geographical Society. Duke of Edinburgh,
Cesarewitch and Count Beust present. Address by Lieut Payer, of Austrian
Arctic Expedition.
Rome. The Pope, receiving several English Catholics, protested against Mr
Gladstone's pamphlet on the Vatican Decrees.
Carlists defeated and compelled to raise siege of Irun, retiring in confusion to
Vera.

Wednesday November 11
Patent of Martini-Henry rifle extended by Judicial Committee of Privy
Council, remuneration of inventor not having been sufficient.

Thursday November 12
South transept of York Minster reopened.
Birth at Staxton, Yorks, of R W Chambers, writer on the English language and
literature (died April 21, 1942).

Friday November 13
Bristol. Annual Colston Banquet.
Hurricane reported from West Indian Islands. Much damage in Kingston,
Jamaica.

Saturday November 14
End of a very cold week. London deaths 1795, 80 more than average
Earl of Derby elected Rector of University of Edinburgh.
Hampstead. Indignation meeting of residents protesting about proposal to
establish a hospital for infectious diseases there.
Death of William Sewell, English divine and author (born Newport, Isle of
Wight, January 23, 1804).

Sunday November 15
Fete day of ex-Empress Eugenie at Chislehurst. Emperor's tomb decorated
with bouquets sent by Bonapartists adherents.
Bonapartists attended Church of St Augustin in Paris in mourning.

Monday November 16
Bank rate raised from 4 to 5 per cent.
Mr Disraeli elected Lord Rector of Glasgow University, his opponent being
Mr Ralph Waldo Emerson.
Oxford. Collins's large carriage manufactory destroyed by fire. Several
houses destroyed. Loss of property approximately £30,000.
Cape Town. Reports that the diamond fields were being kept clear of
water at great expense.

Tuesday November 17
Her Majesty's Government resolved to send an expedition to the
North Pole.
Ship *Gospatrick,* with emigrants for New Zealand burnt at sea in the
South Atlantic. Nearly 300 perished, only three of crew subsequently
rescued.
Arrival of Marshal Bazaine at Madrid.
Sinking of steamer *Empire* at Philadelphia through overloading, 30 lives lost.
Birth at Croydon of B H Streeter, theologian and divine, (died Sept 10, 1937).

Wednesday November 18
Cape Town. Reports of a deep and wide crack in the South African
diamond diggings which threatened to bury all claims.
Birth at New York of Clarence Day, author ('Life with Father' and other
books) died Dec 28, 1935.
Birth at Danton, Ohio of H M Lydenberg, librarian, translator and editor,
died April 16, 1960.

Thursday November 19
Terrible catastrophe on Clyde. A 12-oared cutter belonging to HMS *Aurora*
run down by Dublin steamer *Duke of Leinster.* Eighteen on board thrown
into water and drowned.
Master engineers and shipbuilders on Clyde met and resolved to enforce
general reduction in wages from 5 to 10 per cent.
St Denis nr Paris. Explosion caused by chemicals blowing up. 400,000 fr
damage. Railway station and other buildings damaged. Some casualties.

Friday November 20

Crystal Palace. Shareholders' meeting to consider charges of mismanagement and extravagance against directors. Chairman declared proceedings untimely.

Explosion at Rawmarsh Colliery near Rotherham, 23 killed.

Gazette reported award of Victoria Cross to Capt Mark Sever Bell for gallant conduct during the Ashanti War.

Death of Tom Hood, British humorist and editor of 'Fun', son of Tom Hood the poet (1799-1845) born at Wanstead January 19, 1835.

Death of Archduke Karl Ferdinand of Austria, age 56.

Saturday November 21

Queen arrived at Windsor Castle from Balmoral.

Duke of Edinburgh visited establishment of Messrs Kirkman and Co, Soho Square to inspect an invention of Signor Caldera of which they are patentees, for sustaining sounds of the pianoforte.

Death at Rome of Mariano Jose Bernardo Fortuny, Spanish painter (born at Reus June 11, 1838).

Sunday November 22

Queen and Princess Beatrice travelled to London to be sponsors at christening of son of Duke and Duchess of Edinburgh, visiting Empress of Russia at Buckingham Palace.

The christening scene at Buckingham Palace of the first-born child of the Duke and Duchess of Edinburgh.

Monday November 23
Christening of infant son of the Duke and Duchess of Edinburgh by the
names of Alfred Alexander William Ernest Albert. Sponsors, Queen
Victoria, the Emperor of Russia, the Prince of Wales, the Crown Prince
of Germany and the Duke of Saxe-Coburg-Goths.
Bank rate raised from 4 to 5 per cent.
South Wales ironworkers, agreeing to a 10 per cent reduction in wages,
notice of which expired on Saturday the 21st, went to work as usual.
Slight earthquake shock in Caernarvonshire and Anglesea.
Rome. Opening of Italian chambers by King Victor Emmanuel II.

Tuesday November 24
Empress of Russia, Cesarewitch and Grand Duke Alexander with
Duke of Edinburgh left Buckingham Palace. Empress embarked later for
Paris and the South.
Brighton. Horse, donkey and goat show. First prize won by a horse that
was in the charge at Balaclava and had been owned 18 years by its
exhibitor.
Manchester. Conference of ministers convened by British Temperance
League. Papers read on protection of youth from the evils of drink.
Birth at Malda, Lower Bengal, of Sir Atul Chandra Chatterjee, Indian
Civil Servant and League of Nations Official (died Sept 8, 1955)
Birth of Merle Johnson, American cartoonist and biographer of Mark
Twain (died, 1935).

Wednesday November 25
Sharpness Point, Glos. New docks, costing £200,000 opened.
Dean and Chapter of Worcester Cathedral persisted in their refusal to
grant use of Cathedral for future musical festivals.

Thursday November 26
Dean Stanley elected Rector of St Andrews University.
Rome. Cardinal Manning visited Pope. Discussed Mr Gladstone's pamphlet
and course to be pursued by Catholic Church on this question.
Berlin. First service in the Old Catholic Church, 300 present.
Death of Vice Admiral Joseph Denman, aged 64.

Friday November 27
Probable date of birth at Motol in Pinsk, prov of Grodno of Chaim
Weizmann, Chief Rabbi in Great Britain and Zionist pioneer (died
Nov 9, 1952)

Saturday November 28
Queen held a council. Various foreign diplomats introduced.
Cesarewitch and Grand Duke Alexis visited Opera, Paris.
Birmingham. Opening of annual exhibition of fat cattle, sheep and pigs.
Queen was a successful exhibitor.

Sunday November 29

London. Inventors' Institute, St James's Hall. Sir Antonio Brady advocated reform of the patent laws.

Paris visited by one of the most violent storms experienced.

Severe gales round British Isles, 21 lives lost off Scottish coast; several ships blown ashore. Steamer *La Plata* bound from Thames to South America foundered off Ushant. About 60 believed drowned.

Serious flooding in Nottinghamshire and Derbyshire.

Hyde Park. Several thousand Irishmen demonstrated on anniversary of execution of 'Manchester Martyrs' (executed 1867) and demanded release of Fenian prisoners.

Death of the Hon John Meredith Read Ll D, Chief Justice of Pennsylvania, age 77.

Birth at Crayford Kent of Francis Dodd, painter and etcher (died March 7, 1949).

Birth in India of Sir George Russell Clerk, diplomatist and ambassador, (died June 18, 1951).

Monday November 30

Bank rate raised from 5 to 6 per cent

Birmingham. Great National Exhibition of Dogs at the Curzon Hall (closed Wednesday, December 2).

Dundee. Lord Borthwick lectured to working men on the process by which savings were capitalised and of the financial relations between Britain and the rest of the world.

Social Science Association. Animated debate on Mr Hare's scheme for creating a municipality for London. Nobody in the meeting favoured a continuation of the present conditions.

Church discipline. In the Court of Arches Sir Robert Phillimore held to be illegal the use of candles at morning service if not for giving light, or processions with the picture of the Virgin, the singing of the Agnus Dei, the use of the sign of the Cross in the presence of the congregation, of wafer bread, the cope the chasuble and alb in the communion service. One clergyman, the Rev Mackonochie was suspended and ordered to pay costs.

Birth at Blenheim Palace, Oxon of Sir Winston Spencer Churchill. (died January 24 1965).

december

Tuesday December 1
Princess of Wales's 30th birthday
Quebec Institute. Miss Emily Faithfull gave a glowing account of New
Zealand as an emigration field for females.
Philosophical Institution. Mrs H Fawcett spoke on 'The Woman in
Modern Fiction.'
Meeting of Aborigines Protection Society, London. Discussion on the
abuses of the system of providing coolie labour.

Wednesday December 2
Prince of Wales proclaimed Grand Master of the Freemasons of
England at the Freemasons' Hall, Queen Street.
At the *Turnhalle,* Kings Cross, display given by the German Gymnastic
Society to a crowded hall.
Dr Edward Baughan Hyde Kenealy, leading Counsel for the Tichborne
claimant, disbarred by the benchers of Grays Inn for his extreme and
violent conduct at and after the trial.
Greenwich. Sentence of 21 days' hard labour passed on a man for having
kissed a young woman in a train while passing through a tunnel.
Argentina. Gen Mitre surrendered to Gen Arias. Civil war ended.
Death of Col John Maclean, formerly Governor of Natal, aged 64.
Death of Watts Phillips, novelist, dramatist and artist, aged 45.

Thursday December 3
Queen received a deputation from the French nation with a testimonial
of gratitude and addresses from towns and communities in France in
recognition of the services rendered by the English nation to the sick and
wounded during the war of 1870 - 1.

Queen distributed medals to eight seaman and marines for bravery in the Ashanti campaign, and later gave a dinner at Windsor Castle.
Japanese troops evacuated Formosa.

Friday December 4
Sandringham. Prince of Wales gave a ball to tenants in celebration of birthday of Princess of Wales.
City of London. Possession of Columbia Market returned (on the spot) to Baroness Burdett Coutts through her advisers, by the Comptroller on behalf of the Corporation of London.

Saturday December 5
Rt Hon Benjamin Disraeli suffering from an attack of gout.
Berlin. Prince Bismarck spoke in Reichstag, accusing Pope of desiring French victory, and asserting that it would be no use having a diplomatic representative at Vatican.

Sunday December 6
Versailles. Grand religious ceremony. Public prayers offered on behalf of National Assembly.
Death in Paris of Egide Charles Gustave Wappers, Belgian painter (born Antwerp, August 23, 1803).
Birth at Cedarville, New Jersey of Samuel A K Wilson, neurologist, (died London May 12, 1937).

Monday December 7
Visit of ex-Empress Eugenie to Queen at Windsor Castle.
Meetings at Hollybush Tavern and Albert Hall, Kentish Town, to protest against scheme to erect a hospital for contagious diseases at Hampstead. Metropolitan Asylums Board had refused to abandon scheme.
Opening of Smithfield Cattle Show.

Tuesday December 8
Ex-Empress Eugenie left Windsor Castle.
Islington. Public meeting to promote education among women. Chairman Sir Sidney Waterlow MP.
USA. Unsuccessful attack on Vicksburg by 700 negroes. 25 killed and wounded, 40 taken prisoner.

Wednesday December 9
Transit of Venus observed from various places in the world. New Zealand — obscured by clouds. America — photographs of ingress obtained. Adelaide — ingress cloudy; egress well observed. Peking — hazy, slight black ligament. Tschifu, north-west China — observation highly successful.
Berlin. Commencement of trial of Count Arnim, late Prussian Ambassador in Paris.

Death of Ezra Cornell, founder of Cornell University, New York, age 68.

Thursday December 10
Shoreditch Town Hall. Public meeting to receive report of Epping Forest
Fund Committee. Gratitude expressed to Corporation of London for
efforts to preserve the Forest for use of the public.
Stroud Election Petition. Mr Baron Pigott considered that bribery by
agents had been proved and that Brand, the sitting member, should
be unseated.

Friday December 11
Death of Lt Col George Henry Grey, Equerry to the Prince of Wales,
age 39.
Death of William Urquhart Arbuthnot, Member of the Council for India,
age 67.

Saturday December 12
Parliament prorogued until February 5, 1875.
London Bridge. Suggestions being made in public for widening, with
protecting shelves 12 feet wide on both sides to accommodate the flood

Landing oranges at London Bridge for the Christmas market. **107**

of pedestrians. Mr G Colleton Rennie, son of Sir John, the builder of the bridge, suggested the widening of the approaches.

'The only son of ten children of J W de Foe of Chelmsford and great-great-grandson of Daniel Defoe — such are the credentials on a canvassing card of a poor little boy who is candidate for admission to an asylum of idiots at Colchester.' (Illustrated London News, Dec 12).

Washington. Arrival of Kalakua, King of Hawaii. (See Feb 12).

Sunday December 13
Bishop Colenso inhibited by Bishop of London from preaching in St James's Chapel.

Monday December 14
30th anniversary of death of Prince Consort. Royal family assembled at Windsor, visited mausoleum at Frogmore where Dean Stanley, Dean of Windsor preached the sermon.

Wreck of steamship *Delfina* with loss of 19 lives (Valparaiso) and of *Mongol* with loss of 16 lives (Hong Kong).

Funeral of the Duc de la Rochefoucauld-Bisaccia, former French ambassador in London and friend of the Prince of Wales.

Tuesday December 15
A body of Shakers ejected from New Forest Lodge nr Lymington.

Bristol. Great gathering at Colston Hall to protest against introduction of Romish practices in the Church of England.

Plymouth. West of England Fat Stock Exhibition. Unusually high quality of exhibits.

Heavy fall of snow in London. Thaw which set in the forenoon made streets almost impassable.

Dublin. Lord-Lieutenant of Ireland received a deputation from Provost and Board of Trinity College in favour of higher education for women.

Wednesday December 16
Mansion House. Meeting of Council of Hospital Sunday Fund. Collections had been held at 1,300 places of worship. Total receipts £29,678 -13-2. Expenses £926-17.

Dundee. Meeting of leading citizens to consider scheme for establishment of a college. Intended to raise £150,000 to endow six chairs and secure an affiliation with St Andrews University.

Angers, France. Collapse of market hall roof through weight of snow, Some fatalities.

Thursday December 17
London. Foundation stone of new hall for Carriers Co laid by Master, Mr E S Norris.

Aberdeen. Causewayend Rag Factory burnt down. Estimated damage

£10,000.

Mayor of Grimsby presented two gold medals from the French government and two from French Aeronautical Society to the captain and mate of the fishing smack *Grand Charge* for rescuing M and Mme Durouf from their balloon in the North Sea. (See August 30).
Bismarck's resignation refused acceptance by German Emperor.
Japan. Pacific mail steamer on voyage from Yokohama burnt. Two passengers, surgeon, several sailors and 400 Chinese missing.
Death of the Rt Hon John George Milles, Lord Sondes, age 80.
Death of the Rt Hon Sir John Trollope, Lord Kesteven, age 74.
Birth at Berlin (later Kitchener) Ontario, of William Lyon Mackenzie King, Canadian Prime Minister (died July 22, 1950).

Friday December 18
Queen arrived at Osborne from Balmoral.
Mansion House. Lord Mayor presided over a meeting in which preliminary steps were taken to establish on the Thames a training ship for boys for the merchant service. Approval of the Board of Trade already received.
Hogarth's picture 'The strolling players in a barn' destroyed by fire at the mansion of the Wood family at Littleton, nr St Anne's (painted 1741).
Sale of Mr Gilbey's herd of Jersey cattle at Hargrave Park, Bishops Stortford, a herd 'which ranks as the best and most successful dairy herd in the kingdom.'
Berlin. Chamber passed a vote of confidence in Prince Bismarck.

Saturday December 19
'We are informed that the Midland Railway Company intend to have warming footpans put into all third class carriages and to have the seats cushioned' (Morning Post).
Count Arnim sentenced to three months' imprisonment for having embezzled documents. (See October 4).
Birth at Dulwich, of Sir Clement D C Hindley, railway engineer and public servant (died May 3, 1944).

Sunday December 20
St Pancras. In a public meeting a resolution strongly condemned the proposal to erect a hospital for contagious diseases close to Hampstead Heath. Petitions to be prepared.
Rome. Pope, in a consistory, severely condemned ecclesiastics who had taken part in the last elections to the Italian Chamber of Deputies.
Scutari, Albania. During a storm a powder magazine struck by lightning and exploded. Part of city wall and several houses destroyed. 200 persons killed and injured.

Monday December 21
Marlborough Police Court. Miss Stride, who had incurred heavy liabilities for the maintenance of her Home for Young Women was allowed £30 from the poor box of the Court towards her expenses for the ensuing year.

Malta. Tidal wave rose and fell four feet in ten minutes. Many steamers parted from their moorings.

Tuesday December 22
Windsor. Bishop of Oxford consecrated St Stephens Church.

Wednesday December 23
Death at London of Rt Hon John, 1st Baron Romilly, late Master of the Rolls, (born January 10, 1802).

'Christmas time forty years ago' was the title of this drawing that appeared in The Illustrated London News of 1874.

Thursday December 24
The Queen distributed gifts at Whippingham School and to others on her Osborne estate.
Prince of Wales distributed Christmas gifts at Sandringham to 200 families, of Christmas cheer, beef etc.
Fearful disaster on Great Western Railway at Shipton, nr Oxford; 34 killed, 70 injured.
Explosion at Bignal Hill Colliery. 17 killed.

Friday December 25
Fatal railway accident, Springs Branch, nr Wigan.
Northern Ireland. 'The Shutting of the Gates of Derry' passed off without any disturbance. Effigy of the 'traitor' Benjamin Lundy, which had been suspended all day on a gallows, burned amid great enthusiasm.
Brussels. Deputation of colliers from Charleroi given audience by King of Belgium. Deputation desired that men should have the opportunity to work in the pits of their choice if available.

Saturday December 26
Bank Holiday. Almost total cessation of business in London.
News of a circular from Lord Chamberlain to managers of theatres on the subject of improper dances and dresses. His Lordship expressed the determination to put a stop to all such abuses.
Birth at Holbeach, Lincs of Sir Norman Angell, political writer (died October 7, 1967).

Sunday December 27
Queen, Prince Beatrice and the Duke of Connaught attended divine service at Osborne. Rev George Connor, Vicar of Newport officiated.
Prince and Princess of Wales, Prince George of Wales, the Duke and Duchess of Edinburgh attended divine service at Sandringham Church.

Monday December 28
Innocents Day celebrated at Westminster Abbey. Special service for children, Dean Stanley preaching 'a service suitable to his congregation.'
Craven Chapel, Soho. 200 'poor foreigners' given supper by Mr and Mrs George Moore. After the meal the Rev A Kinnaird, MP took the chair and addressed the meeting briefly in French.
Birth of Max Huber, Swiss lawyer, and representative on various League of Nations Commissions.

Tuesday December 29
Chelsea. Meeting presided over by the Hon F Maude. Resolutions condemning the 'eastward position' and other ritualistic practices in the Church of England.
Spain. Don Alfonso proclaimed King Alfonso XII at Murviedo by General Martinez Campos.

Death at Jersey City of Morgan Lewis Smith, American general (born Oswego County N Y March 8, 1822).

Wednesday December 30
Consols, highest price 93^3/$_8$; lowest 91¼.
The Rev C H Spurgeon presided at Annual Meeting of Pastors' College connected with his Tabernacle. A subscription bust of him unveiled.
Death of Benjamin Attwood, anonymous donor of £1,000 cheques to numerous charities.
Death of Duke of Montrose, Lord Lieutenant of Stirlingshire, age 75.
Death of Ludwig Dessin, German actor (born at Posen December 15, 1810).

Thursday December 31
'From tomorrow there will be only two classes on the Metropolitan Railway. Fares: 1st class, 1½d a mile; 3rd class unaltered. Return fares at reduced prices to be abolished.'
Death of Col Thomas Walter Millward CB. Aide-de-camp to the Queen, age 50.
Death of Alexandre Auguste Ledru-Rollin, French politician and rebel (born Fontenay-aux-Roses, Seine, February 2, 1807).
Birth at Liverpool of Holbrook Jackson, essayist, died June 15, 1948.